DAVID STEVENS

GARDENS BY DESIGN

IDEAS FOR SMALL GARDENS

BBC BOOKS

Published by BBC Books,
A division of BBC Enterprises Ltd,
Woodlands, 80 Wood Lane, London W12 0TT

First published 1990
© David Stevens 1990
ISBN 0 563 21572 0
Reprinted 1991

Typeset in 10 on 13 point Futura
by Ebenezer Baylis & Son Ltd
The Trinity Press, Worcester, and London
Printed and bound in Great Britain by
Ebenezer Baylis & Son Ltd
The Trinity Press, Worcester, and London

CONTENTS

ACKNOWLEDGEMENTS

Roger Beckett
Lightscape Projects
67 George Row
London SE16
for lighting.

Capel Manor Institute of
Horticulture and Field Studies
Bullsmoor Lane
Enfield
Middlesex
and Nick Evans for all their help.

Jardinerie Garden Centres Ltd
Bath Road
Haresfield
Gloucestershire
and Paul Cooper for their fitted garden.

ARC CONBLOC
P.O. Box 14
Appleford Road
Sutton Courtenay
Abingdon
Oxon OX14 4UB
for their hospitality and use of gardens.

Laser Creations Ltd
55 Merthyr Terrace
Barnes
London SW13 9DL
for lasers.

IBSTOCK BUILDING PRODUCTS LTD
180 Albany Street
London NW1 4AW
and special thanks to Roger Ellingworth
and Peter Clark for their help with the
computer graphics.

Cramphorn plc
Cuton Mill
Chelmsford
Essex CM2 6PD
for their sponsorship of the 'Lovers' Garden'.

Individual Gardens Ltd
271–273 High Street
Berkhamsted
Hertfordshire HP4 1AA
for use of their offices.

The National Trust
for their assistance at Stowe.

and all the people who gave their time
and gardens so willingly and kindly.

To the following designers:
John Brookes
Alex Dingwall-Main
Julie Toll
Jill Billington
Paul Cooper
Richard Key
Judith Close-Smith
Debbie Roberts and Ian Smith

And finally, a very special thanks to Victor Shanley

PICTURE CREDITS

Front cover photo John Glover, design
Duane Paul Design Team, and pages 33
(top left) photo Brian Carter, RHS Chelsea
Flower Show 1987, design Geoff & Faith
Whiten/Halifax Building Society, (top
right) photo Ron Sutherland, Rob Herwig
Garden, Holland, 35 (right) and 36 photo
Brigitte Thomas The Garden Picture
Library; 33 (bottom) 34, 37 and 38 Photos
Horticultural, Michael Warren; 35 (left)
Impact Photos, Pamela Toler; 39 Jessica
Strang; 40 (top and bottom) David
Stevens; 74 (top left) BBC; back cover
photo Richard Bryant ARCAID.

Copyright for illustrations and plans
Paul Cooper, pages 78 and 79; Will Giles
and Sandra Pond, pages 19, 32, 46 and
47 (original design © Julie Toll, 52, 53,
59, 65, 84, 85, 92 (right) (original design
© David Stevens), and 96 (original design
© David Stevens); Donald Grant, pages
74–75; Individual Gardens Ltd, pages 56,
58, 60, 61, 62, 63, 67, and 68; Debbie
Roberts and Ian Smith, page 80; David
Stevens, pages 28, 29, 43 and 44, and
92 (left); Julie Toll, pages 24, 72 and 73,
and 88; Jill Tomlin, pages 76–77.

INTRODUCTION

GARDEN DESIGN IN THE PAST

The history of garden design is directly linked to the history of the development of man. From the very earliest 'hunter/gatherer' societies man started to protect himself within enclosed areas and, before long, plants that were grown for food were also included in these areas. As time went on such spaces took on a rectilinear form and were protected by walls or hedges. Water and irrigation also became an increasingly important feature as plants began to be grown for a wider variety of purposes; for food, ornament and shade (particularly important in the hot countries surrounding the Mediterranean where many early civilisations flourished).

Gardens, similar to those we know today, were first introduced into Britain by the Romans. Set within the house itself, like a courtyard surrounded by four walls, these 'atriums' were genuine outside living rooms; a style that is now being reproduced in contemporary garden design.

With the destruction of the Roman Empire, monasteries continued the development of the garden within the shelter of the cloisters, with the cultivation of herbs for cooking and medicine. Slowly, as time went on, fortification became less important and the garden began to develop in a more decorative, though still formal pattern. Gardens in Britain never achieved the grand scale of those on the Continent and only really started to come into their own in the eighteenth century when a unique and dramatic flowering of design ideas resulted in the birth of the English landscape garden. This has become our only truly indigenous contribution to the history of garden design.

Three names dominated garden design in that period: William Kent, 'Capability' Brown and Humphrey Repton, all of whom strove to create an idyllic landscape of trees, water and grassland that swept right up to and surrounded the great houses of the day. Just such a park still exists, largely intact, at Stowe in Buckinghamshire. Although apparently unrelated in size and style to present-day gardens, many of the design techniques and features to be seen are still, in fact, of use to us today. The overall theme of simplicity, the use of vistas to focus on a distant object and the clever use of drives that meander through the estate to increase the apparent size of the grounds, are all valuable 'tricks of the trade' used by today's garden designers, albeit on a greatly reduced scale. Even the use of temples and other focal points has a direct link with contemporary garden ornament and, although it would be a little strong to call Stowe the Gnomeworld of the eighteenth century, the simile is in many ways apt!

AN EXTRA 'LIVING' ROOM

Unfortunately, but inevitably, the landscape garden has passed away, replaced by ever smaller spaces that have to serve an increasing range of activities. Today's garden is indeed an outside room and, as such, the emphasis on gardening has shifted. No longer is it a place in which to toil over vegetables or to stake vast borders of herbaceous plants. It is a place where the family can relax, a place for play and entertainment, a place for taking and cooking meals and a place for doing household chores. How much more pleasant are all these activities when done outside?

WHY DESIGN?

Most of us expect to plan the rooms inside our home; we are able and happy to choose wallpapers, colour schemes and fabrics, and to position furniture so it has sensible access and enough space around it. It is also true that good interior design is now readily available both through High Street stores and a wide range of practical publications. However, as soon as we move outside the story is rather different, the ideas dry up, we become confused, we resort to impulse buying and it is little wonder that the garden ends up as a jumble of unrelated features that are difficult to maintain and have little chance of serving us in a coherent manner. In part, this is due to the mystery that still surrounds plants; not only are those long Latin names confusing, but many of us fail to understand the limitations of sun, shade, and different types of soil. Garden centres and nurseries also tend to compound the problem with an almost endless array of walling, paving, plants, pools and ornaments. Sensible advice is difficult to get and although some retail outlets offer garden design services, the majority do not. Most seem only interested in selling you their products – the way in which these end up in your garden is of little consequence to them.

The reasons for designing a garden should be straightforward; you wish to create something that suits you and your family well, can adapt as circumstances and requirements change, looks good throughout the year and, perhaps most important, serves you and not the other way round. You should never be a slave to your room outside.

A well-planned garden will allow you to allocate a budget over a period of time, it will prevent you wasting hard-earned cash by placing plants and features in the wrong place, it will almost certainly put value on your property and it will make your house easier to sell than a house with a poorly designed garden.

HOW THIS BOOK CAN HELP YOU

This is not a gardening book in the conventional sense. There is nothing here about growing vegetables, pruning plants or using weedkillers; all these, and similar subjects, are covered in ample detail elsewhere. Instead, this book is about how to organise your outside room, how to choose the fabrics (the paving, walling and planting) and how to integrate features and furnishings so that they look a part of the overall composition rather than an afterthought that has been simply tacked on. This book will help you rationalise your thoughts and assess the needs of your family and, most important, it will ensure that your garden fits you like a glove, reflecting your own unique personality and that of your family.

There should be no sense of mystery about garden design or designers, they are simply people who have learnt their craft and know how to get the best from the space that adjoins your home. Designers come in all shapes and sizes with different styles and ideas. This book will help you to choose one that suits you, your pocket and also suggests how you can make the most of him or her.

On the other hand, if you wish to design your own garden, this book will not only show you the techniques that the professionals use but will also offer you simple guidelines that will make the job a whole lot easier.

1

A PROFESSIONAL APPROACH OR DO IT YOURSELF?

USING A DESIGNER

Many people think of design and designers in terms of 'glossy magazines'; probably too expensive and certainly flighty. All-in-all, pretty unattainable. In fact, nothing could be further from the truth. Most designers work from a well-tried and tested set of rules that have been learnt from many years of experience. Their fees are usually moderate and will almost certainly be less than an architect's.

For the average garden measuring, say, 15m × 15m (50ft × 50ft) the fees for a design and planting plan would be in the region of £300–£400; the price of a thousand bricks, a dining table or an armchair. This fee and the experience it brings will in all probability save you many times this amount in mistakes and wasted time. It will, in effect, give you an additional room and that alone is worth a good deal.

A designer's job is to interpret what *you* want and not to impose his or her ideas on you. There is nothing worse, or wasteful, than a designer that simply does their own 'thing'. You then have their garden and not yours. A designer should be on your wavelength, understand what you want and be able to mould it into a sensible, no-nonsense plan. If you want the fancy and outrageous stuff there are certainly designers who can provide it, but remember that something that may be initially startling may quickly pall.

If you do choose to employ a designer, bear in mind that they can only produce a plan around what you tell them, so think very carefully about what you want before they come. Think also about what you *don't* want as this can be just as important. Also, while many people's conception of a well-designed garden springs straight from a magazine page remember that the garden has to contain the ugly as well as the beautiful. You will need to tell your designer about the shed and the greenhouse, the compost heap or incinerator, the washing line and dustbin.

The great advantage of employing a designer is that they are trained to interpret what you want whilst at the same time paying attention to the good and bad points of your site. They will know what is worth keeping or removing, be able to check soil types and have the ability to recognise plants. Designers will also be able to work out constructional details for any features involved, obtain quotes from reputable contractors and oversee work in progress so that, at the end of the day, you are completely satisfied with the final result. They can do as little or as much as you want. Perhaps, however, one of the best reasons for employing a designer is that they will simply be able to cast a completely fresh eye over the subject which you may have become bogged down in looking at day-in and day-out.

On the debit side, a designer's time will have to be paid for and their fees will either be charged on an hourly rate, to include travel, consultations and the production of drawings, or as a fee negotiated at the start of a job. As with all professional people, and garden designers are just that, ascertain exactly what you are in for and obtain a written quotation first.

Of course, you don't have to employ a designer to carry out a complete scheme, you can simply buy several hours of his or her time. Such an approach can be invaluable for plant identification, projected growth, condition of trees, soil testing and to advise on just what will grow where. Most designers can also supply you with standard lists of plants for sun, shade, screening, damp and so on, from which you can make your own choice later on. (Such lists are included at the back of this book.) This same approach can be applied to lawn-care programmes, the planting of a specific bed or a suitable combination of fruit trees for a small orchard. If you already have an established garden you can still seek a designer's view on how a layout can be improved or modified. Such guidelines can get you thinking and working in the right direction.

However, for whatever size of job you employ a designer, it is essential that you have a real rapport with them. If you don't get on, then it is best to say so right at the start – it will save not only misunderstandings but a great deal of hard cash!

USING DESIGN SERVICES

A major cost of employing a designer on a personal basis is the time taken by them in travelling to and from your site and in chatting over your problems and requirements. Obviously this will provide a genuinely personal service but it will certainly need to be paid for. A cheaper alternative would be to use a postal planning service like those run by a number of national magazines, certain nurseries and garden centres, and some major DIY retailers. The basis for all these services is a pre-printed questionnaire (probably something like the one overleaf) that asks you exactly what you have got in your garden already and what you want. This will involve a basic survey which can be plotted onto graph paper. Photographs are also helpful and are usually returned to the owner together with the finished plans. Fees are usually on a sliding scale, depending on the size of the plot, and you also usually have the choice of just having the basic garden layout, or this and a full planting plan. Remember, too, that one of the advantages of working to such a plan is that once you have it you can remain faithful to the original concept, however long the actual construction takes.

I have been running such postal services for the past twenty years and they have become increasingly sophisticated. We now offer a 'Maintenance Guide' that not only identifies every plant in the garden but also tells you, on a month-by-month basis, just how it should be tended.

Such services can never have the personal touch of a visiting designer but are extremely good value for money and, once you have your plan, it can either form the basis for quotations from professional landscapers or the starting point for a DIY project which you can undertake over a period of time.

One small point to bear in mind is that the demand for postal services

GARDENS BY DESIGN

Client name

Level of maintenance

Are you a keen
gardener?

Average gardener?

Ages of children

Lazy gardener?

Any pets?

What will your
garden mainly be
used for?

What do you have?

What do you want?

- [ ] Changes in level
- [ ] Soil type
- [ ] Good or bad views
- [ ] Manholes
- [ ] Existing paved areas
- [ ] Existing plants/trees

- [ ] Terrace/patio
- [ ] Summerhouse
- [ ] Rockery
- [ ] Built-in barbecue
- [ ] Bin screen
- [ ] Play area
- [ ] Soft fruit
- [ ] Roses
- [ ] Lawn
- [ ] Greenhouse
- [ ] Pond/pool
- [ ] Pergola
- [ ] Dog run

- [ ] Swings/slide
- [ ] Herb bed
- [ ] Fruit trees
- [ ] Veg plot-large/small
- [ ] Shed
- [ ] Rockery with stream
- [ ] Arbour
- [ ] Sandpit
- [ ] Washing line (type)
- [ ] Annuals
- [ ] Herbaceous
- [ ] Anything else

Anything else?

Anything you don't want?

tends to be seasonal. Everyone wants their garden planned in spring when the turn-round time can be six weeks or more, by which time half the summer may have gone! Think of getting the garden planned in the autumn or early winter, it can then be built in good time for the coming season.

I have included a list of magazines offering postal planning services and professional design bodies on page 110 if you wish to pursue either of these methods.

A third possibility is now becoming increasingly available when you buy a new home. A number of enlightened developers are starting to offer free garden plans as part of the purchase deal. This usually involves a visit by a qualified consultant who checks out your requirements and sends them into the design company who carry the work out. Such services are a hybrid between a freelance designer and a postal service and there is no doubt that they are immensely helpful to anyone moving home. Some developers are at last even starting to offer 'fitted gardens', and why not, everything else in the house is fitted! This is the way ahead in the future – it can only be a relatively short time before such gardens are the norm.

DESIGNING IT YOURSELF

However you have your garden planned, whether it be through a garden centre, a postal planning service or employing a designer, it will cost you money. There is no doubt that it will be money well-spent and it could save you a great deal of time. On the other hand, however, there is absolutely no reason why you should not plan the garden yourself, as long as you follow a sensible sequence. Just what that sequence is we will be laying-out step-by-step in this book.

By the time you've finished this book you should be in a position to design your own garden. Remember, though, that you will often need further information on construction before you attempt to build some of the more complicated features mentioned – this is primarily a book on design principles and ideas, not a manual on how to build a garden.

2

WHAT HAVE YOU GOT AND WHAT DO YOU WANT?

It can be difficult enough for a professional designer to remember all the points that a client raised and the exact nature of a garden. It will be even more difficult for you, the DIY designer, to get your thoughts into a logical pattern, something which is essential if the design is to be successful. It can therefore be invaluable to work out a check list of all the items and features that you already have in the garden and then to list all the things you want to see in the finished design. In other words to work out what you've got and what you want.

By asking these two questions you have immediately broken the design process down into two quite separate stages, the first will involve a simple survey and the second, writing a check list. However, before you write your list of what you want, such things as budget and maintenance have to be considered and these will be looked at later in this chapter.

WHAT HAVE YOU GOT?
DOING A SURVEY

Surveying is not the complicated job it's made out to be by architects and other professionals, but to carry it out properly you do need the rudimentary tools of the trade; a tape measure 30m (100ft) long, a clipboard, paper, pencil, a number of bamboo canes and a simple child's magnetic compass.

Start by just drawing out the shape of the house, the position of doors, windows and the garden boundaries. Then mark in any existing features such as trees, established planting, hedges, walls, and garden buildings, such as a shed or greenhouse. An established patio should be shown, as well as any paths, drains, manholes or hard standing areas.

As far as planting is concerned it is worth noting everything, however unlikely. A gnarled old hedge may seem a hindrance at the time but could form a useful screen later on. It's also worth bearing in mind that many plants die down in winter so you may need to survey the garden in spring when they are starting to show above the ground. Bulbs too come into this category – it would be a shame to dig through or plan an area only to find it full of dormant plants or bulbs.

Next run the tape measure across the rear of the house, fixing it to the fence or holding it down with one of those canes. Leave the tape in position and read off the measurements in sequence, jotting them down as you go. Thus you might have the corner of the house, the start of the patio doors or the French windows, the other side of the doors, the position of the kitchen window and so on, until you reach the opposite boundary. Before you reel the tape in just go back and check that you have remembered everything, the manholes for instance or the position of that drain.

Now fix the tape against the rear of the house and run it down the garden until you reach the bottom boundary. Go back and repeat the measurements in this direction noting the end of a patio, the position of a tree, where the shed is and so on. If the tape does not reach all the way down the garden, read off the measurements as far as it goes, mark the end with another cane and start again.

If there is a slope try and estimate this. Steps are easy enough to measure and so is the height of a retaining wall. It can also be possible to look back from the bottom of the garden, pick a point on the house at eye-level, measure it and work out the change in height. This latter technique will not be accurate to the last millimetre or inch but it will be close enough in most garden situations. If, however, a garden is large, has vicious slopes and cross-falls compounded by trees or buildings, and disappears around a dog-leg, then it is a job for a professional surveyor – and the fee will be well worth it!

GOOD AND BAD VIEWS

Many people tend to underestimate the importance of a good or bad view. If you are lucky enough to have the former, a glimpse of a distant tower, the rooftops of a village below or the view of a fine landscape, then make sure that you mark the necessary details on your survey plan. More often than not, unfortunately, the view is not so good; the next door garage, a neighbour's house overlooking your patio, an ugly factory and so on. All is not lost, however, as these can easily be screened, but only if you indicate where they are so that you can blot them out later on.

SOIL

The soil that you have in your garden will determine just what you can grow. It is divided into two broad layers; topsoil which is fertile and subsoil which is not. Topsoil is supposed to be just that, the surface layer of soil, but unfortunately some builders still cover it with subsoil, dug from the foundations of the house. If they do this then get them to remove it *before* they disappear off site. Where topsoil is concerned it can range from either a sticky, heavy clay soil or quite the opposite and very sandy. Most soil can be improved by the addition of organic matter in the form of compost, well-rotted manure or leaf mould. Peat is also an excellent soil conditioner, but I for one would not now use it in this context owing to the environmental problems associated with its extraction.

Soil will also range from either acid or alkaline (chalky) and this, too, will determine just what you can grow. An acid soil, for instance, is essential for rhododendrons, azaleas and many (though not all) heathers. To make the best of your garden you will need to check this with a simple soil-testing kit or meter that you can buy at your local garden centre. Take samples from several places in the garden as readings can vary, particularly if some of the soil has been imported by the builder.

SHELTER

It is wind, more than any other factor, that prevents us using the garden in this country. Note the direction of any prevailing wind or any persistent draught that blows around your garden, perhaps deflected by adjoining houses. Such a problem will be easily overcome by the sensible siting of a screen or wall when you come to do the design.

ASPECT

The most important survey job I have left to last; the passage of the sun throughout the day. The position of sun and shade will not only determine just where you sit but also what plants will flourish where. Make a note of where the sun rises and sets and remember that the length of the shadows will vary enormously in summer and winter. If the day is cloudy use your compass to check the exact alignment of north and south, bearing in mind the sun rises in the east and sets in the west. It can be useful to mark where the sun rises, its path during the day and where it sets, on your drawing. Also, mark the direction of north clearly.

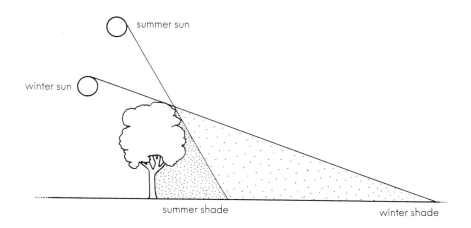

summer sun

winter sun

summer shade   winter shade

WHAT DO YOU WANT?

THE CHECKLIST

By now you will have a pretty good idea of the shape, size, limitations and advantages of your plot and are in a good position to start thinking about what sort of garden you want and what sort of features to include in it. The easiest way to do this will be by compiling a check list. This is a family job, after all, that valuable 'living room' is going to be used by everyone. A typical list might include patio or terrace, barbecue, a water feature of some kind, lawn, room for swings or slide, planting, shed, greenhouse, paths, hard standing for a boat or caravan and so on. Remember too that the garden has to include the siting of dustbins, washing line, compost heap and incinerator which will also need to be thought about and included on your list. Don't worry if the list seems endless, you can always thin it down later. The important thing is not to leave anything out; it can be very difficult to incorporate a major feature once the garden is complete and such an addition usually looks like an afterthought. However, before you start writing your list make sure that you read to the end of the chapter. There are a few other points worth thinking about.

WHAT IS YOUR BUDGET?

There is absolutely no point in designing a garden, or even putting together a check list of what you want to see in the finished scheme, before you have a realistic idea of what you want to spend.

Most people, and this includes the majority of garden writers and broadcasters, seem to think that a worthwhile garden can be built on a shoestring. While one can certainly keep a budget to a sensible minimum, it is still fair to say that the cost of most constructional work, if carried out by a competent landscaper, will be broadly similar to employing a builder. Even on a DIY basis, the cost of plants and materials can mount up and this makes a good working design doubly important.

An average garden measuring, say, 15m×15m (50ft×50ft), landscaped and built for you professionally will cost about £7500 or as much as an average family saloon. The big difference is that as soon as you drive a car out of the showroom it devalues whereas a garden does the exact opposite. It will almost certainly put value on your property and make it a good deal easier to sell when you come to move. Some banks and building societies are now even lending money, on a home improvement basis, for gardening construction. It could be well worth a call to your local branch to check this.

Of course you don't have to spend the full budget figure right away. The great value of working to a design means that you can carry the job out in stages and thus spread the cost over a period of time without losing sight of the original concept.

In broad terms the 'hard landscape' of a garden, that includes paving, fencing, walling, paths and other major features such as barbecue, raised beds and water features, will take the lion's share, up to 75%, of the total budget. 'Soft landscape' (that includes lawn, trees, shrubs and ground cover) is relatively inexpensive and, despite what anyone says, plants are still exceptionally good value for money.

HOW LONG WILL YOU STAY?

It is a fact that the job market these days is a good deal more fluid than it used to be and this means that people move home rather more often. Such moves can on average be every five years or so and, in gardening terms, this means people simply do not have the time to see a garden develop from scratch. A truly 'instant' garden is not really a possibility, although they are built at the Chelsea Flower Show. However, the use of more mature stock and the selection of fast-growing species that knit together quickly can make a tremendous impact in a relatively short period of time. Many garden centres and nurseries are fully aware of this trend and in consequence offer large plants to achieve this effect. Such plants are by no means cheap, but you have to remember that you are paying for several, and in some cases, many years of growth. If you need a garden to mature quickly then you should make a sensible allocation in your budget to purchase at least a framework of larger plant material.

LEVEL OF MAINTENANCE

Perhaps one of the most important questions you should ask yourself is just how much time you and your family have to spend on maintaining the plot once completed. In short, are you a keen, average or lazy gardener? If you are the last there is no shame attached – so am I! But, if this is the case, you will need to plan things that require the minimum amount of ongoing work. Think carefully about this, a large lawn can often be more work than a well-planned border carpeted with ground-covering plants that knit together and form a carpet. A rockery may sound attractive but usually involves a high level of care to just keep all those pockets of soil free from invasive weeds.

WHAT DON'T YOU WANT?

One final point, and something that we always ask as professional designers – what don't you like? This is desperately important, particulary if you are using a postal planning service or employing a designer. Most common on the list is poisonous plants, particularly where young children are present. It can also include specific colours of flowers, the choice of plants, an aversion to a particular kind of paving, the inclusion of water and so on.

The compilation of your check list should be done over a period of time. You will inevitably remember things as you go along, and while you are doing it, keep your eyes open, see what you like in other people's gardens, save clippings from magazines that show features or specific plant groupings that you find attractive. All of this will allow you to start building up a picture of the finished garden in your own mind. Just how you can start to translate all these thoughts into hard fact we shall look at in the coming chapters.

3

MAKING A SITE PLAN

You may have felt that all the preparation was a bit long-winded, but it is vital to go through these basic stages before putting pen to paper. It is a sad fact that even so-called professional landscape gardeners attempt to produce designs quite literally on the back of an envelope. Regardless of the possibility that the aesthetic input may be suspect, it is quite impossible to prepare any scheme properly unless the garden has been drawn to scale.

It is also true that by using a controlled approach over a period of time you have not only allowed the family's ideas to crystallise but you have also been able to see just what the existing garden has in the way of plant material that may not have been initially visible.

To prepare a site plan, which will be the basis of your design, you will need a square of A3 or larger graph paper, several sheets of tracing paper, tape to stick the various sheets down, pencil, rubber and, of course, the survey drawing that you have already carried out.

1 First stick the sheet of graph paper onto a flat, smooth surface with sellotape or draughting tape – a drawing board is obviously ideal for this.

2 Position tracing paper over this and stick down in a similar manner.

3 Now choose a suitable scale. A scale simply means that the squares on the graph paper represent a certain distance or area on the ground. In other words a certain number of squares will represent 1 metre (or 1 foot).

4 Now, from your survey drawing, work out the rough size of the plot so you know just how big the finished drawing is going to be. Once you know this you can start by positioning the house at the bottom of the sheet of tracing paper. Now transfer the rest of your measurements from the survey drawing to your new site plan remembering to keep to scale. It is probably safest to use pencil at this stage.

Plot all the measurements of the house, types and position of boundaries and also work out where any additional features are, such as planting, trees

GARDENS BY DESIGN

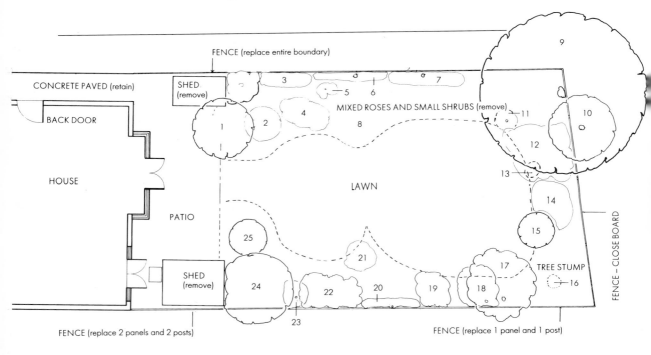

FENCE (replace entire boundary)

CONCRETE PAVED (retain)

SHED (remove)

BACK DOOR

3

5   6

7

9

MIXED ROSES AND SMALL SHRUBS (remove)

11

10

1

2

4

8

12

HOUSE

13

14

PATIO

25

15

LAWN

21

17

TREE STUMP

24

18

16

SHED (remove)

22

20

19

23

FENCE – CLOSE BOARD

FENCE (replace 2 panels and 2 posts)

FENCE (replace 1 panel and 1 post)

SITE PLAN OF THE JONES'S GARDEN – BEFORE

1 1 dessert apple tree (existing – remove)
2 1 ground-cover juniper
3 1 variegated ivy
4 4 evergreen azaleas
5 1 pieris (existing – retain)
6 1 vine bearing purple edible grapes (existing – retain)
7 1 honeysuckle
8 Mixed roses and small shrubs (existing – remove)
9 1 hawthorn (existing – retain)
10 1 culinary pear tree (in neighbouring garden)

11 1 cotoneaster (existing – remove)
12 1 lilac (existing – remove)
13 1 *Berberis thunbergii* (existing – remove)
14 1 pyracantha (existing – remove)
15 1 skimmia (existing – retain)
16 Ivy-covered tree strump
17 1 pyracantha (existing – retain)
18 1 escallonia (existing – retain)
19 1 *Berberis thunbergii* 'Atropurpurea' (existing – retain)

20 1 honeysuckle
21 1 *Hebe anomala*
22 1 *Viburnus tinus* (existing – retain)
23 1 *Jasminum nudiflorum* (existing – remove)
24 1 *Cornus alba* (existing – remove)
25 1 camellia (existing – retain)

(and perhaps the area of shadow they cast at different times of the day or year), a sharp change of level, the position of existing paving, the manholes and so on. This is the time to indicate the position of neighbouring houses and the windows that may overlook you and also to put in an arrow for the direction of the prevailing wind. Mark any spots in the garden that you may have found were waterlogged at a particular time of the year. Did you remember to mark that glimpse of a church spire or distant chimney and how about the ugly garage that may be in full view of a proposed patio?

The last job, as it was on your survey drawing, is to mark in the direction of north and south. It can again be a good idea to mark the path of the sun with an arc that moves across the top of the plan.

You will probably find this slow going to start with, but take your time and nip outside to check any measurements you may have forgotten – the home designer has a definite advantage over the professional who has to get all the measurements right first time! Don't be afraid to use your rubber, this is the designer's most valuable tool. There is nothing worse than a scale drawing that is a mass of conflicting lines, none of which are quite in the right place – it only leads to disaster later on!

5 When you have transferred all the measurements from the survey to your scale site plan and you are happy that the one faithfully represents the other you can go over the pencil in ink. This will make the drawing permanent and allow you to rub out the underlying pencil work.

6 Once the scale drawing is complete take plenty of photocopies, or trace some more copies. The first site plan you work on will soon be reduced to a complete jumble of conflicting and meaningless lines so make sure you only use a copy. File the original away for safe-keeping.

Opposite is the site plan that the designer, Julie Toll, made of the Jones's back garden in the television series. It is fairly typical of any such plan. Later on we shall see the hard-landscaping and planting plan that Julie designed for the Jones's (page 88) and finally an illustration of what the garden will look like when it is established (pages 76–7).

4

PLANNING: THE OVERALL PATTERN

Now that you have completed the scale drawing of your plot as it is, you can start to think about the actual plot you want – the creation of a special environment to fit you and your family like a glove. That, of course, is one of the most important criteria of any design; your requirements will be quite different from anyone else's, and that will make your garden unique. In short, it is personality that shapes gardens and that is why you should never simply copy a design from a book, a magazine or a friend's plot. Take ideas, by all means, seek inspiration, certainly, but at the end of the day mould these with your own thoughts and needs to produce just what you want.

Once your check list is complete, you can start to put the items into sequence with the most important features at the top. This will help you get your priorities right and if the list is too long you can start to see which items might be left out. In other words, a patio and lawn could be of more consequence than an asparagus bed or a rockery. On the other hand, you might be an alpine enthusiast, in which case a rockery or scree garden could feature high on the list.

At this stage you need only think of roughly allocating space. For example, the main paved area for sitting and dining, provided it caught plenty of sun, would probably be outside the patio doors or French windows with reasonable access to the kitchen. However, if this position was in shade for much of the day, you would think of siting the main terrace elsewhere, bearing in mind a path or some kind of paving would be necessary to link it back to the house. Certain features also have a generic role to play; dustbins, an oil tank or a wood store could be grouped together in a well-designed single store, with both easy access for servicing and the house. In the same way other 'utility' features like the compost, the incinerator, the shed or storage area could also be grouped together. To separate all of these would not only lead to visual confusion but would also involve endless tramping around the garden to get from one to the other. As with a patio, access will again be important so mark in the line of a possible route on your plan to make sure you can get to all those items and back to the house dry shod.

As a general rule, the smaller the garden the more important this approach is. Always remember that the most important design rule is simplicity; try to keep to it, even with the mundane items.

BASIC PRINCIPLES OF DESIGN

Design is an often misunderstood word. It can best be described as the moulding of ideas and features into a sensible and simple whole. Overleaf is an example of a well-designed small garden (Jon and Verna's garden in the television series) which combines a number of the basic principles of good design. Overcomplication is the antithesis of good design but it is something from which far too many gardens suffer. Simplicity brings with it a degree of constraint and this in turn imposes a sequence of planning that not only prevents confusion but gives the complete composition continuity. In basic terms, design is the creation of patterns and those patterns can be organised and planned in just the same way as you would tackle interior decoration inside the home.

The house is a logical starting point for any garden design as the building already has an architectural pattern which should be reflected in the paved areas, paths or patio that surround it. Here you can use a series of interlocking rectangles that project from the corners of the house or pick up the line of doors or windows. Crisp rectangular precast slabs, solid pieces of natural stone, or the pattern of brick paving, will all be perfect for reinforcing that link between house and garden.

Other factors can come into play here too, a colour scheme inside the house can be continued out along an adjoining wall, or plants can be grouped on either side of the glass of patio doors, masking and softening the division between inside and out.

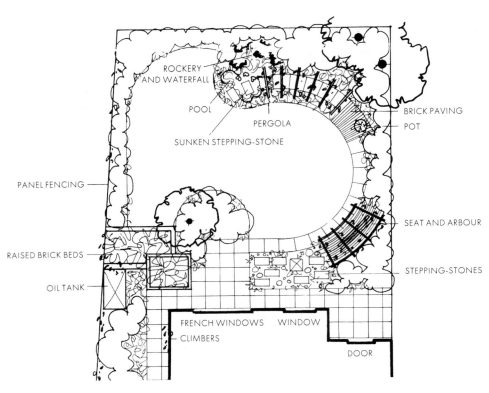

ROCKERY AND WATERFALL

POOL

PERGOLA

SUNKEN STEPPING-STONE

BRICK PAVING

POT

PANEL FENCING

SEAT AND ARBOUR

RAISED BRICK BEDS

STEPPING-STONES

OIL TANK

FRENCH WINDOWS   WINDOW

CLIMBERS

DOOR

JON AND VERNA'S GARDEN

1 1 *Phormium tenax*
2 1 Azaleas – Japanese
3 1 *Pieris* 'Forest Flame'
4 7 *Erica carnea* vars
5 1 *Juniperus virginiana* 'Skyrocket'
6 2 *Hydrangea hortensia*
7 1 *Philadelphus* 'Virginal'
8 2 *Spiraea* 'Goldflame'
9 3 *Geranium endressii*
10 1 *Cotinus coggygria* 'Royal Purple'
11 1 *Clematis montana* 'Rubens'
12 1 *Robinia pseudacacia* 'Frisia'

13 2 *Santolina chamaecyparissus*
14 2 *Buddleia davidii* 'Royal Red'
15 1 *Weigela florida* 'Variegata'
16 1 *Jasminum officinale* 'Affine'
17 1 *Acer palmatum* 'Atropurpureum'
18 7 Alpines – mixed
19 11 Alpines – mixed
20 10 Alpines – mixed
21 1 *Cotoneaster horizontalis*
22 1 *Kerria japonica* 'Pleniflora'
23 1 *Pyrus salicifolia* 'Pendula' (specimen)

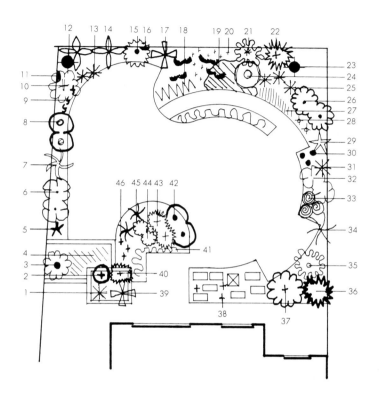

24	1	*Paeonia lactiflora*
25	3	*Geranium* 'Johnson's Blue'
26	2	*Philadelphus coronarius* 'Aureus'
27	17	Annuals
28	2	*Iris sibirica* 'Perry's Blue'
29	1	*Spiraea arguta*
30	3	*Geranium* 'Johnson's Blue'
31	1	*Cytisus scoparius* 'Andreanus'
32	2	*Hydrangea hortensia*
33	3	*Hosta* 'Thomas Hogg'
34	1	*Tamarix pentandra*
35	1	*Deutzia* 'Mont Rose'

36	1	*Arundinaria murielae*
37	1	*Viburnum opulus* 'Sterile'
38	3	*Astilbe simplicifolia* 'Sprite'
39	1	*Acer palmatum* 'Atropurpureum'
40		*Juniperus squamata* 'Blue Carpet'
41	9	Annuals
42	2	*Hebe subalpina*
43	2	*Euonymus fortunei* 'Emerald and Gold'
44	2	*Lavandula spica* Hidcote'
45	2	*Genista lydia*
46	3	*Geranium sanguineum*

Disjointed materials like crazy paving tend to be visually unstable and while they may be fine for an informal sitting area towards the bottom of the garden, tempered by grass and planting, they are often too restless to adjoin the building.

Increasing distance from the house brings informality. In the middle and more distant parts of the garden you can start to use strong flowing curves that not only lead the eye away from those almost inevitable rectangular boundaries but provide a real feeling of movement which can in turn create a feeling of greater space.

SCALE

Scale, in garden design terms, means the overall relationship between the plot and the house, and the relationship of the internal features with one another. In other words, a large house with a tiny garden would seem out of scale as would a vast expanse of paving surrounding a diminutive lawn. Scale is all about proportion, balance and a feeling of 'rightness' that is essential to any good composition.

In practical terms this means that you should think about the size of a particular feature and the space it requires in relation to the other parts of the garden. Too many small features produce a restless, busy pattern and this is one reason for thinning down your check list to a realistic level. The principle works the other way as well; I once planned a garden for a golfing fanatic who wanted the maximum area for driving lightweight balls. The end result was bland in the extreme.

Scale should not only relate to the area within the boundaries but also to what is beyond – a good view or the proximity to dominant buildings. In the case of the latter it can make sense to soften and balance the line of these with well-positioned trees, or break the view with overhead beams run out from the house and defining a sitting area below. If you are lucky enough to have a fine view of rolling countryside then your garden pattern should reflect this by using soft curves, carefully placed planting to frame the vista and, perhaps, earth shaping or contouring to echo the view in the garden.

FOCAL POINTS

Focal points are the punctuation marks of a garden; too many of them and the design becomes fussy, too few and the composition lacks interest altogether. Also bear in mind that visual show stoppers like a gigantic rockery, overflowing with colour, can look contrived – any focal point worth its name is better left underplayed and subtle. A well-positioned seat, for example, set in an informal sitting area on the far side of a garden will naturally draw the eye and perhaps open the space up on a diagonal to make the garden feel larger than it really is. A statue or urn can act as a full stop at the end of a pergola or highlight a doorway into the house, while a pool creates a point of interest within a paved patio area.

In other words, look at your overall plan, see where you wish to create interest and relate these focal points to one another.

THE DIFFERENCE BETWEEN FORMAL AND INFORMAL

Formal and informal are words that are often used in relation to garden design but seldom fully understood. A formal design relies on symmetry so that one side exactly reflects the other. This style can reflect the architecture of the house or can be used as a quite separate 'set piece' in a different part of the garden altogether, perhaps surrounded by walls or hedging. Such layouts are often suitable for a balanced collection of plants, of roses, or herbs for example, or perhaps a composition that relies on specific colour combinations. The layout is essentially static but this does not mean it is without interest. Formal gardens do, however, tend to be impractical in a family setting.

Informality is a dangerous word and covers a multitude of sins. A better definition is asymmetrical. This kind of garden is altogether more flexible but at the same time just as carefully conceived. The essence of an asymmetrical design is balance rather than a mirror image and can be likened to the position of heavy and light weights either side of a fulcrum. In garden design terms this means that the visual weight of a paved area to one side of the

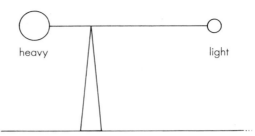

When balancing 2 objects of different weights on a fulcrum, the heavier object must be nearer the centre than the lighter one. The same principle is true in a garden – a more prominent feature should be visually balanced with a less prominent feature.

garden could be balanced by a specific group of trees or a sweep of planting on the other. Alternatively a small but well-detailed pattern of paving or planting could be offset by a larger simple shape.

The essence of good design, as we are starting to see, is that it looks and 'feels' right; this applies to a garden in the same way as it does to a painting, a fine building or a suit of clothes.

USING CURVES

As we have seen, the importance of using rectangular shapes close to the building was to reinforce the link between house and garden. Further down the garden, however, curves will come into their own to produce a more fluid pattern that provides that vital feeling of space and movement.

All too often gardening books tell you to work out the shapes of borders by flinging a garden hose on the ground, kicking it about a bit and then cutting out the shape with a spade or edging iron – DON'T! The best way to work out curved features like borders or paths is to draw them on the plan using a pair of compasses. Starting from a straight line draw a series of curves that link into each other using different radius points. When these are softened by planting, the overall effect will be just right. They can be simply transferred onto the ground by using a stake as the radius point of the circle and swinging a line from this, marking out the curve as you go.

Left: *Gravel is an excellent foil for planting, which can be allowed to grow and self-seed through the surface. Contrast in size and texture is provided by pebbles and small boulders (see page 59).*

Right: *Brick is an attractive and versatile paving material. The stretcher bond seen here tends to lead the eye onwards, creating movement (see page 60).*

Above: *The brick of the patio area is continued in the raised beds. Notice how well the neat timber seat adds contrast to the brick yet still harmonises with it. Luxuriant planting can disguise any hard lines or angles (see page 68).*

Right: *Conservatories make a wonderful link between house and garden, particularly where planting is massed on either side of the glass. Make sure the style of the conservatory respects that of the house (see page 70).*

Opposite: *A pergola and trellis are used to soften a bad view. Both provide excellent support for climbing plants which will increase the screening effect (see page 65).*
Left: *A good summerhouse like this one is an attrative focal point in a garden. Most look best when softened with a background of planting (see page 70).*

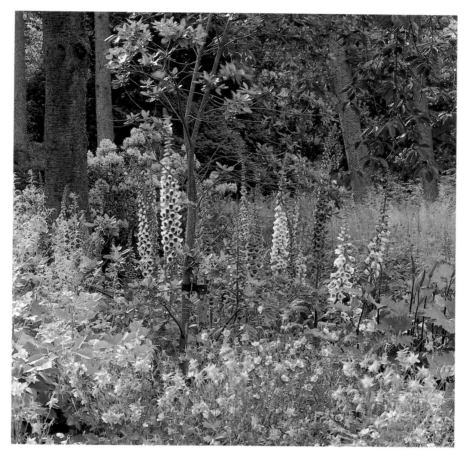

Above: *If you require a low-maintenance garden, it is often best to follow the principles of nature, like this woodland garden does (see page 84).*

Opposite: *Positioning of any ornament is all-important. As with this one, they often look best slightly tucked away and surrounded by planting (see page 81).*

Above: *When planting a garden, simplicity is all-important.*
White has been used in this part of the famous Sissinghurst garden to provide
continuity throughout the composition (see page 86).

Opposite: *Although not the easiest of gardens, a roof garden can be*
a delightful haven in an urban environment (see page 98).

Above: *My own front garden (see page 96).*
Below: *My own back garden (see page 91).*

SHELTER

We have already mentioned that it is often a lack of shelter that prevents us from sitting outside and for this reason it is important to note the direction of prevailing winds on your site plan. From this it will be easy enough to position a wall, fence or screen of planting to help reduce the problem.

NOISE

Noise, or how to deal with it, is often completely overlooked in garden planning, but certain steps can be taken to at least reduce the impact of an adjoining road or busy playground. A dense screen of plants can be effective, particularly if set on a gently contoured bank.

Another solution, in a specific area such as a patio, is to create a diversion by introducing another noise. The gentle sound of running water from a pool or similar water feature can do much to blanket an intrusive sound. Thus, make sure you mark in the approximate position of any necessary screening or feature.

BACK AND FRONT GARDENS

All too often both developers and designers tend to think of these as having separate identities. In fact, as long as you provide reasonable privacy by sensible siting of your various garden features, there is no reason why the garden should not flow around the house, providing far greater continuity and helping to make the overall garden feel a great deal larger than it might perhaps be. The point is, of course, that there is no need for items traditionally sited in the back garden to be there at all; dustbins are far more appropriate in the front garden close to the street, and why not have an ornamental pool surrounded by planting in a well-thought-out, structured pattern right by the front door, acting as a focal point. Neither would it be impossible, provided there was ample space and adequate screening, to have the main sitting area in the front, if this was the only place that caught the sun for most of the day. Remember, think laterally!

GARDENS BY DESIGN

DRAWING THE PLAN

What we have just been looking at are some of the principles of design. What you now need to do is combine these with your own ideas and translate them into a finished plan. The materials you will need to do this are a copy of the site plan that you prepared earlier on tracing paper, pencil, rubber, ruler or set square, and a simple child's compass.

The grid you used to work out the site drawing can also be used to work out the design. Stick the grid down and lay a copy of your site plan over this so that the graph paper shows through the tracing paper and lines up with the house. It can be sensible to start the design of a paved area from the corner of the house or the edge of the French windows or patio doors. Thus for a terrace area you can work out the paving pattern over the grid by allocating one, or a number of squares, to each slab depending on your scale. In this way you can build up a pattern of different kinds of paving, say a combination of precast slabs and brick, as well as other features such as raised beds, built-in seating, a barbecue or a pool.

There is no need to always think of a patio being square with the house, you can sometimes turn the whole pattern to an angle of, say, 45°. This will immediately lead the eye away from the shape of a rectangular plot and by using diagonal lines (the longest distance across a rectangle) you help to provide a greater feeling of space.

As I said earlier, do draw the design roughly to begin with, allocating space in general terms. Don't try to finish the scheme right away, leave it if you get stuck, get the family to look at it, and slowly the positioning of features will become firmer as the composition is honed down to a clean, sensible pattern that will work in both visual and practical terms.

DIFFERENT SHAPED GARDENS

Gardens come in all shapes and sizes, long, narrow, square, wide, dog-leg and so on. All the things that you want will need to be fitted in somewhere but the shape of the plot can make a big difference as to the final pattern.

42

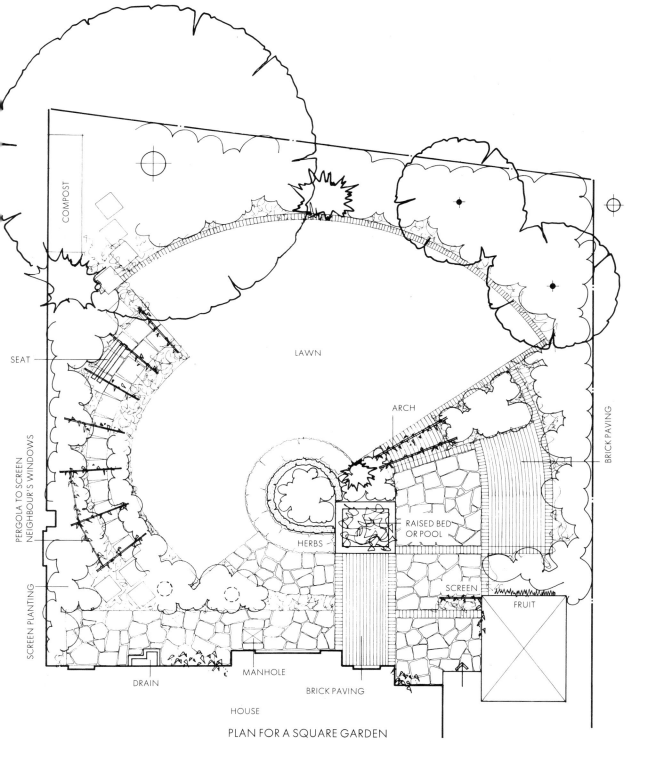

COMPOST

SEAT

PERGOLA TO SCREEN
NEIGHBOUR'S WINDOWS

SCREEN PLANTING

LAWN

ARCH

BRICK PAVING

HERBS

RAISED BED
OR POOL

SCREEN

FRUIT

DRAIN

MANHOLE

BRICK PAVING

HOUSE

PLAN FOR A SQUARE GARDEN

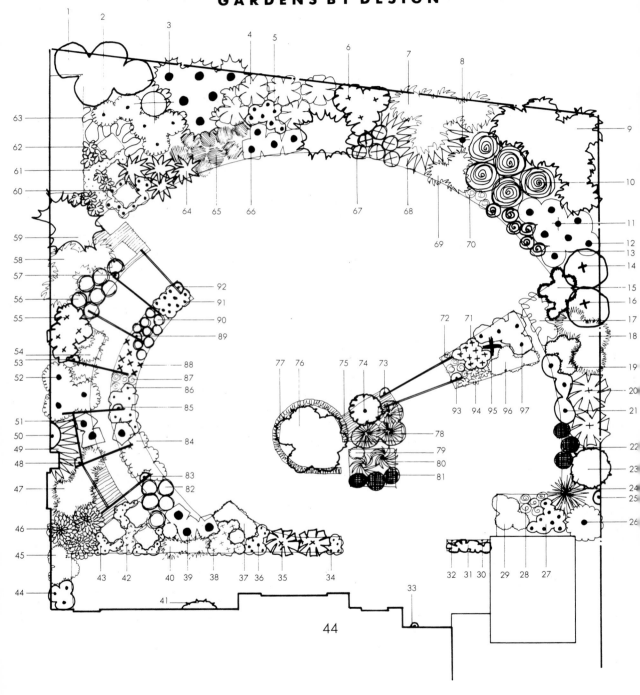

44

SQUARE GARDENS

Where long gardens have visual movement in a given direction, square plots are absolutely static. If you have a view out of the garden it will be a great help to lead the eye towards this by the alignment of planting or the direction of a path. By doing this your vision jumps beyond the boundaries and this helps to break down the shape.

If, however, there is nothing but fences or walls then the pattern may well have to turn in on itself, a circular shape perhaps, focusing on a centrally placed feature. One such design can be seen on page 43 together with a planting plan opposite. Alternatively you might think of emphasising the garden's shape by building up a composition of overlapping squares and rectangles, part with paving, part with grass or gravel, with planting to fill in the gaps in between and soften the outline.

1 4 *Aucuba japonica* 'Variegata'	**33** 1 *Hedera helix* 'Gold Heart'	**64** 4 *Sarcococca confusa*
2 5 *Symphoricarpos chenaultii*	**34** 4 *Hebe pinguifolia* 'Pagei'	**65** 9 *Skimmia japonica* 'Rubella'
3 6 *Mahonia japonica*	**35** 2 *Viburnum plicatum* 'Mariesii'	**66** 4 *Euonymus fortunei* 'Emerald
4 5 *Fatsia japonica*	**36** 7 *Hebe pinguifolia* 'Pagei'	and Gold'
5 7 *Polygonatum hybridum*	**37** 6 *Santolina chamaecyparissus*	**67** 6 *Viburnum davidii*
6 3 *Escallonia* 'Apple Blossom'	**38** 8 *Aquilegia* 'McKana Hybrids'	**68** 20 *Geranium endressii*
7 4 *Cornus alba* 'Elegantissima'	**39** 3 *Euonymus fortunei* 'Emerald	**69** 3 *Spiraea bumalda* 'Anthony
8 1 *Prunus* 'Tai Haku'	and Gold'	Waterer'
9 6 *Elaeagnus angustifolia*	**40** 2 *Juniperus squamata* 'Blue Star'	**70** 3 *Hosta sieboldiana*
10 5 *Cotinus coggygria* 'Royal Purple'	**41** 1 *Rosa* 'Golden Showers'	**71** 9 *Crocosmia masonorum*
11 1 *Prunus* 'Tai Haku'	**42** 9 *Lamium maculatum* 'Beacon	**72** 5 *Hosta sieboldiana*
12 7 *Hypericum patulum* 'Hidcote'	Silver'	**73** 1 *Rosa* 'Meg'
13 6 *Bergenia purpurascens*	**43** 23 *Ajuga reptans* 'Atropurpurea'	**74** 1 Existing rosemary
14 1 *Syringa vulgaris* 'Katherine	**44** 3 *Helleborus orientalis*	**75** 6 *Geranium* 'Johnson's Blue'
Havemeyer'	**45** 3 *Potentilla fruticosa*	**76** 7 Hybrid tea roses
15 8 *Berberis thunbergii*	'Katherine Dykes'	**77** 30 *Lavandula spica* 'Hidcote'
'Atropurpurea Nana'	**46** 3 *Choisya ternata*	**78** 3 *Cytisus kewensis*
16 1 *Syringa vulgaris* 'Madame	**47** 5 *Deutzia* 'Montrose'	**79** 1 *Potentilla davurica* 'Abbotswood'
Lemoine'	**48** 1 *Parthenocissus henryana*	**80** 2 *Genista lydia*
17 5 *Stachys lanata*	**49** 15 *Lupinus* 'Russell Hybrids'	**81** 3 *Cistus* × *lusitanicus* 'Decumbens'
18 3 *Kolkwitzia amabilis*	**50** 1 *Jasminum nudiflorum*	**82** 5 *Fuchsia magellanica*
19 5 *Potentilla fruticosa* 'Princess'	**51** 3 *Euonymus fortunei* 'Gaiety Silver'	**83** 1 *Hydrangea petiolaris*
20 2 *Viburnum tinus*	**52** 3 *Philadelphus coronarius* 'Aureus'	**84** 5 *Hebe* 'Autumn Glory'
21 3 *Sedum* 'Autumn Joy'	**53** 1 *Lonicera periclymenum* 'Belgica'	**85** 1 *Lonicera periclymenum* 'Belgica'
22 3 *Cistus* 'Silver Pink'	**54** 5 *Spiraea* 'Gold Flame'	**86** 6 *Euphorbia polychroma*
23 1 *Rosa moyesii* 'Geranium'	**55** 4 *Hydrangea macrophylla* 'Blue	**87** 4 *Hosta* 'Thomas Hogg'
24 1 *Cytisus albus*	Wave'	**88** 7 *Astilbe*
25 1 *Rosa* 'Swan Lake'	**56** 7 *Fuchsia magellanica*	**89** 1 *Clematis tangutica*
26 1 *Philadelphus* 'Virginal'	**57** 1 *Clematis* 'The President'	**90** 9 *Dicentra spectabilis*
27 8 *Schizostylis coccinea*	**58** 3 *Cornus alba* 'Spaethii'	**91** 10 *Iris foetidissima*
28 5 *Hosta fortunei* 'Albopicta'	**59** 20 *Geranium* 'Johnson's Blue'	**92** 1 *Clematis* 'The President'
29 4 *Potentilla fruticosa* 'Mount	**60** 10 *Hypericum calycinum*	**93** 1 *Rosa* 'Schoolgirl'
Everest'	**61** 12 *Saxifraga umbrosa*	**94** 4 *Hebe pinguifolia* 'Pagei'
30 1 *Clematis montana* 'Alba'	**62** 8 *Euphorbia robbiae*	**95** 1 *Buddleia globosa*
31 4 *Helleborus niger*	**63** 12 *Helleborus corsicus*	**96** 4 *Potentilla fruticosa* 'Tangerine'
32 1 *Hydrangea petiolaris*		**97** 4 *Euphorbia griffithii* 'Fireglow'

SLOPING GARDENS

Sloping gardens are neither easy to handle or cheap. The creation of steps, retaining walls and intermediate level areas can involve both considerable hard work and a large budget.

The garden opposite (shown in the television series) rises just over 2m (6½ ft) from the back of the house to the rear boundary and presented a considerable challenge to the designer, Julie Toll. Immediately adjacent to the house is a sitting and dining area of ample size, floored with neat precast concrete paving slabs. A built-in seat and raised pool provide a delightful focal point and the small fountain adds background sound and movement to the composition.

Steps climb from one side of the terrace and a diagonal path leads across the garden helping to open the space up along its longest dimension and increasing its visual size.

Lawn occupies the highest level, while a small shed provides storage for garden tools. Planting softens the entire garden, clothing fences and disguising the line of retaining walls to provide colour and interest throughout the year.

1 2 pyracantha – red berries (existing)
2 1 honeysuckle (existing)
3 1 *Vitis coignetiae* (existing)
4 1 *Amalanchier canadensis*
5 3 *Aubrietia* 'Maurice Pritchard'
6 1 *Cotoneaster dammeri*
7 1 *Cedrus deodara* 'Golden Horizon'
8 3 *Pulsatilla vulgaris* 'Rubra'
9 1 *Ceanothus impressus*
10 1 *Hemerocallis* 'Stella d'Oro'
11 1 hydrangea (existing)
12 1 *Elaeagnus ebbingei* 'Limelight'
13 1 mock orange (existing)
14 1 forsythia (existing)
15 1 *Rosa* 'Madame Pierre Oger' (existing)
16 3 *Scabiosa caucasica* 'Clive Greaves'
  3 *Gentiana sino-ornata*
  3 *Nepeta mussinii*

17 8 *Cotoneaster dammeri* (on bank)
18 1 *Clematis* 'Madame Baron Veillard' (existing)
19 1 honeysuckle (on trellis; existing)
20 1 *Clematis montana* 'Elizabeth' (trained over store)
21 2 pyracantha – orange berries (existing)
22 2 *Cotoneaster dammeri*
23 1 *Clematis* 'Marie Boisselot'
24 1 *Garrya elliptica*
25 2 *Anemone japonica* 'Alba'
26 1 *Euonymus fortunei* 'Silver Queen'
27 1 *Cornus controversa* 'Variegata'
28 1 *Juniperus communis* 'Sentinel'
29 3 *Hedera helix* 'Green Ripple'
30 1 *Rosa* 'Snow Carpet'
31 3 *Hosta* 'Thomas Hogg' (in tub)
32 2 *Bergenia* 'Bressingham White'
33 3 *Polygonatum multiflorum*
34 3 *Molinia caerulea* 'Variegata'

35 1 *Genista pilosa* 'Vancouver Gold'
36 1 *Philadelphus coronarius* 'Variegatus'
37 1 *Hebe pimeleoides* 'Quicksilver'
38 1 clematis – purple (existing)
39 1 *Fuchsia magellanica* 'Variegata'
40 1 *Rosa* 'Nozomi'
41 1 *Juniperus horizontalis* 'Hughe
42 3 *Campanula* 'Stella'
43 1 *Rosmarinus officinalis* 'Miss Jessup's Upright'
44 2 *Campanula lactiflora* 'Prichard's Variety'
45 1 *Cistus* × *corbariensis*
46 1 *Santolina chamaecyparissus*
47 1 *Euphorbia wulfenii*
48 1 *Salvia officinalis* 'Purpurasce
49 3 *Helianthemum nummularium* 'Cerise Queen'

PLANNING: THE OVERALL PATTERN

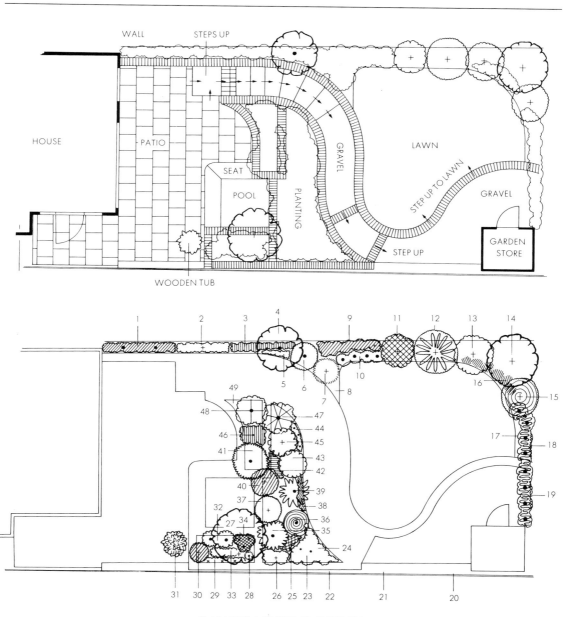

WALL   STEPS UP

HOUSE

PATIO

SEAT

POOL

PLANTING

GRAVEL

LAWN

STEP UP TO LAWN

GRAVEL

STEP UP

GARDEN STORE

WOODEN TUB

PLAN FOR A SLOPING GARDEN

LONG NARROW GARDENS

This is the classic shape of a garden built between the Wars. Unfortunately it is all too often seen with a path running slap down the middle, flanked by a washing line on one side, a border on the other and more borders running parallel to the fences. The result is not unlike papering a tall narrow hall with bold vertical stripes; visually rather uncomfortable.

In fact, long narrow gardens are the easiest to handle as they can be broken down into a whole series of 'living rooms', each one in a more manageable shape and each given over to a different theme. In this way the area nearest to the house could be occupied by the patio, divided from the next by a wall of about 1m (3¼ft) high. The second room could be lawn surrounded by planting, the third perhaps a play area, while the bottom of the garden could be given over to the shed, compost and general utility. Instead of running a path down the middle, start it to one side, turning across the space as you enter the next 'room' and then off down the plot again, in a side to side pattern. This will have the effect of visually widening the garden. I have designed my own back garden along these lines. You can find the hard-landscaping and planting plan for it on page 92.

DOG-LEG

Dog-leg gardens are the kind that disappear off around a corner. All too often the action is concentrated in the first part, with the bit out of sight forgotten altogether. In fact, that feeling of mystery, and wondering just what is around the corner, is one of the vital elements of good garden design – you need to lead both feet and eye into the second space. This can easily be done with an inviting path and the positioning of planting. Once the first room is left behind, the second should hold a promise; a secluded sitting area and arbour, a summerhouse or simply an area of rougher naturalised grass with bulbs and wild flowers and an old seat just waiting to be used.

GARDENS TO ATTRACT WILDLIFE

All gardens attract wildlife to a degree and one has to remember that many so-called pests are just as wild as anything else and deserve a habitat. The point is, of course, that we are becoming quite rightly conscious of our environment and the importance of preserving it.

While a garden can be well-structured and designed it can also be planted to attract a wide spectrum of birds, animals and insects. Such plants as buddleia and sedum are well-known for being able to attract bees and butterflies; lesser known in this connection are ivy flowers; and of course the wealth of berrying plants and trees that are a haven for birds.

In general terms it is a good idea to grow some species that are indigenous to your area. Look around the locality and see which trees and shrubs are growing wild or semi-wild. Not only will these thrive in your garden but they will reinforce the underlying landscape and ecology. A pool will attract frogs, damsel and dragon flies, rougher grass can be sown with wild flowers, a patch of brambles is a good habitat for many small mammals and a few nettles, if kept reasonably at bay, are another attraction for the butterfly. None of these features need detract from the style or purpose of your design, they are simply an adjunct to it and a delightful one at that. One such garden has been designed by Julie Toll for this year's Chelsea Flower Show. 'The Wildlife, Wild Flower Garden' is a superb example of how you can design a beautiful garden that is a haven for wildlife as well. (See pages 72–3.)

The gardens of this country cover a vast area and if everyone did just a little then we could make a very positive contribution to the preservation of our wildlife. Would that more farmers took the same attitude instead of just destroying hedgerows, wetland and other priceless habitats.

5

PLANNING: THE MATERIALS

WHAT MATERIALS SHOULD YOU USE?

The essence of selecting materials for the garden depends on both a respect for local building styles and traditions, and a need to keep the design simple. One of the first problems that faces anyone designing or building a garden is the wide range of choice available. Time was when a local stone was all that you could use for walling and paving, now, however, the local garden centre will be crammed full of every conceivable type of fence, paving and stonework.

In basic terms it should be obvious that to have a concrete screen block wall adjoining a granite Cornish cottage is wrong. Likewise a slate wall in a Cotswold garden would be equally incongruous. Both materials have their place, the point is to make sure they are used in it.

There is no doubt that snobbery also enters into the equation; it may be considered 'the thing' to have Westmorland (Lake District) stone in a Surrey rockery but do bear in mind that it will probably look totally out of place and will also cost a fortune because of transport costs. For a garden to look its best, the materials from which it is built should have some form of positive link with the surroundings.

Very often the house is an excellent starting point, primarily because it is probably the largest single element on the site. If the house is built from brick then it will make sound sense to include the same material in the patio, reinforcing the link between home and garden. The theme could be continued with raised beds, a wall running out from the house and other features such as a barbecue or binstore. Similarly, if you are lucky enough to have a cottage with a stone flagged floor, then what could be more natural than to use a similar material outside.

Of course, not all situations are as clear cut as this. Many houses are rendered and painted, having no real local affinity. In this case the choice is far more open but remember that key rule of simplicity; use materials sparingly but well.

WALLS

Walls can be built from brick, stone or concrete and the prime factor to bear in mind is their suitability and compatibility with the local scene. They are durable but expensive to build and in order to maintain privacy need to be about 2m (6½ft) high. In the front garden remember that there may well be a local authority restriction on the height of walls, often 1m (3¼ft), so if you are thinking of building one it will be wise to check first.

Brick   is the most widely available walling material and comes in a vast range of finishes and colours. As a garden wall is open to the weather on both sides a good, hard facing brick will be essential and, to look at its best, should be built two bricks thick. A final layer of bricks on their side, running crosswise, will prevent weather getting in the top of the wall and a suitable concrete foundation will be essential beneath the ground.

   Single thickness brick walls are cheaper but far less strong, as we have seen in the recent gales. They will need buttressing at regular intervals.

Stone   really only differs from brick in that it is usually available in irregular sizes. It is also invariably more expensive. Stone walls can be laid 'dry' and have an inherently rural feel. For this reason they rarely look at their best away from their natural environment. To build a dry-stone wall takes a degree of skill but the end result is superb. A maximum height of 1.8m (6ft) should never be exceeded. Stone walls can also be built with mortar joints but, if you do this yourself, make sure that the pointing is neat, otherwise it will look ghastly.

Concrete   is much maligned but is, in fact, a useful and versatile material in the garden. Concrete blocks measuring 450×215×215mm (18in×9in×9in) can be used to build a strong and good-looking wall. If the blocks are smooth then they can be neatly pointed and either left as they are or painted to pick up a colour scheme inside the house. If they have a rough finish then they are best coated with cement (rendered) and again painted.

Ornamental screen block walls have unfortunately retained their popularity over the years. They come in a number of patterns that are hard on the eye and offer little in the way of privacy. They frankly look contrived and, if you do use them or inherit them, they are best smothered with a rampant climber.

ORNAMENTAL SCREEN BLOCKS

RETAINING WALLS

Retaining walls are just what they sound like; they hold back a change of level. In design terms they should echo materials used elsewhere in the garden. Construction can be a skilled job and, if they are over 1m (3¼ft) high, should be entrusted to a competent builder or landscape contractor.

FENCES AND TRELLIS

Fences form the majority of garden boundaries in this country. They are relatively cheap, easy to erect and will last up to twenty years if maintained regularly with a non-toxic preservative. NEVER use creosote which is poisonous to plants.

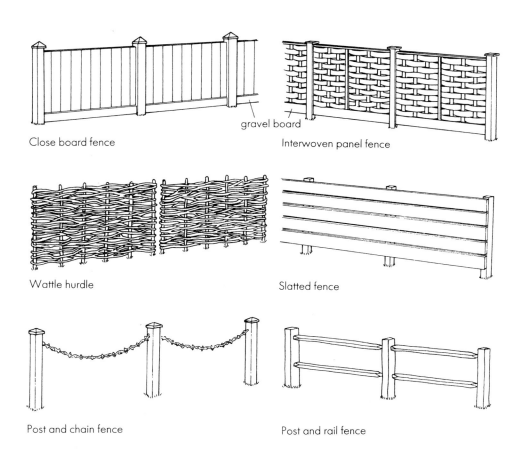

Close board fence

gravel board

Interwoven panel fence

Wattle hurdle

Slatted fence

Post and chain fence

Post and rail fence

Interwoven panel fencing is probably the most common type. It is fixed between concrete or timber posts which are set into the ground. To prolong the life of the fence a 'gravel' board (a wooden plank) should be set between the bottom of the panels and the ground. The gravel board can then be removed if rot sets in.

Close board fences are rather more expensive but last longer than interwoven panels. They take the form of overlapping individual boards nailed to horizontal rails that run between the posts. One advantage is that single boards can be removed in the case of rot or damage. Gravel boards should also be used.

Slatted fences are rather more linear in pattern and instead of the boards overlapping as they do in close board fences they can be spaced with a slight gap inbetween. They associate particularly well with modern houses and can be set either vertically, on rails, or horizontally, between posts. The latter will produce a strong linear pattern that leads the eye in a particular direction.

Wattle hurdles are made from woven hazel stems and were originally used for penning sheep. They are usually available 1.8m (6ft) high and although they have a maximum life of ten years they look superb behind planting. They should be wired onto round posts.

OPEN FENCES

Post and rail is the most common type of open fencing. It is stock proof and consists of either two or three rails set between posts. It affords no privacy but is ideal in a position where you wish to preserve a view.

Post and chain is a traditional urban front garden fence. White timber posts are linked by black wrought iron chain. Anyone using the plastic version should be shot at dawn!

TRELLIS

Trellis is best used as a garden divider and not as a support for climbers on house walls where horizontal strands of wire are far neater. The beauty of trellis is that it allows the glimpse of a view through it – always a tantalising prospect.

There is an increasing range of unusual patterns available on the market that swoop and dive all over the place. While many of these are just about acceptable in an urban garden, they can look pretentious elsewhere. They are a good example of how fashion can rear its head in the garden and, to be honest, do a similar job as those awful ornamental concrete screen block walls that we discussed earlier.

A simple squared trellis, preferably made from hardwood to minimise rot, is an excellent host for climbing plants. Wings of trellis to subdivide a long garden can be delightful, but remember that this kind of structure should be a vehicle for plant material rather than a feature in its own right.

PAVING

Paving is the major hard-landscaping material in the garden and will occupy most of those areas which are used for sitting and dining, access and hard standing. In terms of budget, paving can amount to 75% of the total garden costs so it is vital to choose well and lay it soundly.

As far as a sitting area or patio is concerned, the minimum size should be 3.6×3.6m (12ft×12ft) which roughly equates to an average room inside the home. Paths need to be about 1m (3¼ft) wide and, if laid just below the level of an adjoining lawn, will act as a mowing edge and eliminate that tiresome chore of hand-edging. As we have already seen, paths should link all parts of the garden and, if you have a young family, a circular route will be ideal for wheeled toys.

Where paving adjoins a house the finished level should always be two bricks or 15cm (6in) below the damp proof course and have a gentle fall, or slope away from the building to aid drainage.

As a general rule, natural materials such as stone slabs, cobbles, granite setts (like bricks made of granite) and slate are more expensive than man-made materials. This is due partly to the cost of quarrying and partly to transport charges. On the whole though, natural stone has the beauty of age and will last a lifetime.

The larger a paved area, the simpler a surface should be. A drive or hard standing will look better entirely laid to gravel, concrete or tarmac rather than a conflicting mass of materials. In contrast, a terrace or patio is naturally more intimate and here you can mix and match materials in a straightforward pattern. Remember, too, that the smaller the material you use the easier it is to lay to a curve. Cobbles, brick or setts will conform to a sweeping path while larger slabs would need cutting to shape which is a laborious and costly operation.

The texture of the surface you choose will also affect the speed and type of traffic passing over it. Smooth concrete or tarmac is a high-speed surface, bumpy cobbles are exactly the opposite. In other words, when choosing materials go for those that will look good, suit your requirements and conform to the layout easily.

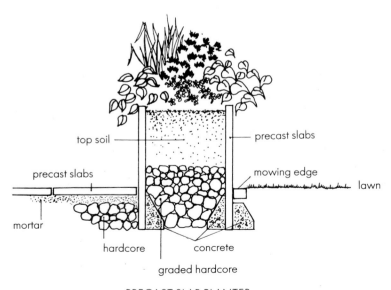

PRECAST SLAB PLANTER

MAN-MADE PAVING

Precast concrete paving slabs are available in a vast range of sizes, shapes, textures and colours. As a general rule, square slabs will look better adjoining a modern building as opposed to a random pattern of different sizes, this latter type being more suited to a traditional setting.

Some slabs are absolutely smooth which again look fine in a modern setting, while others are riven to simulate natural stone, some with excellent effect. Always ensure that any paved area has an adequate foundation of well-compacted hardcore (broken brick or stone), the slabs preferably being laid on five spots of mortar. Slabs can be either fitted together tightly with no joint (butt jointed) or left with a gap and then pointed. If you leave a gap then each slab stands out in sharp relief which can in itself add to the overall design of the floor.

When choosing what colour paving slabs to have, beware of bright colours, they spell visual disaster and fade to a sickly hue. Grey and Cotswold (honey coloured) are generally the best and look fine in most situations.

The link between a paved patio area and the rest of the garden can also be enhanced by making precast slab planters (see diagram).

Concrete blocks are approximately the same size as a brick and are ideal for drives and hard standing, although they are a little too severe for a sitting area. They are laid on sand over a well-compacted bed of hardcore and are extremely durable if the edges are held in position by boards or a line of blocks set in concrete.

Concrete can be cast into large panels up to approximately 3.6m (12ft) square. Don't make your panels larger than this as the concrete may crack. It is a cheap, practical material and should be used more often in the garden but always take care to soften its sometimes harsh effect with careful planting. The main advantage of concrete is that it is 'fluid' and can therefore be cast in curves. It can also be textured in a variety of ways.

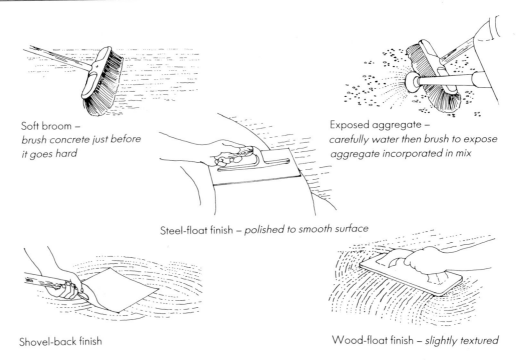

Soft broom –
*brush concrete just before
it goes hard*

Exposed aggregate –
*carefully water then brush to expose
aggregate incorporated in mix*

Steel-float finish – *polished to smooth surface*

Shovel-back finish

Wood-float finish – *slightly textured*

CONCRETE FINISHES

NATURAL MATERIALS

Stone is perhaps the finest and most expensive paving available. York
stone is most widely used and this can come either new, which can look the
same as a good precast slab, or old when it has usually worn into a
beautiful texture. Second-hand stone can be up to 10cm (4in) thick and can
be bedded on mortar on a minimal foundation.

Slate is a fine and sophisticated paving, glistening in the wet and with
superb crispness of line. It should be used in modern architectural situations.

Cobbles are those egg-shaped water-washed stones that you find on the beach. Don't pinch them, it's illegal! They can be laid in patterns and courses and should always be tightly packed so no mortar shows between the joints. As a foil for other materials like old York stone, precast slabs or brick paving, they look superb and their size makes them perfect for a curved path. They can also be used as an 'oil drip' to disguise stains from a car where it regularly stands in a drive.

PATH WITH COBBLE INFILL

Gravel is smaller than cobbles and is ideal for both drives and paths. It is a superb foil for planting which can be allowed to grow and self-seed through the surface (see page 33).

Granite setts were traditionally used for paving streets. A full sett measures about the same size as a brick, a half sett is just what it says. Like cobbles, they can be laid in patterns and can be a useful contrast material within a larger paved area. Being slightly uneven they are not ideal under tables and chairs but this same characteristic makes them ideal for drives.

Brick is one of the most beautiful and versatile paving materials around. It can form the ideal link between house and garden and its small size makes it ideal for laying to a curve. Bricks should be hard enough to stand up to the ravages of frost and an increasing number of manufacturers are now producing clay paving bricks or clay paviors specifically for the garden.

Brick can be laid in a number of different 'bonds', including basket weave, herringbone, soldier courses and stretcher bond (see diagram). Different patterns can have an effect on the overall design, for example, stretcher bond laid down a path leads the eye on (see page 33), while the same bond across the path tends to be more static.

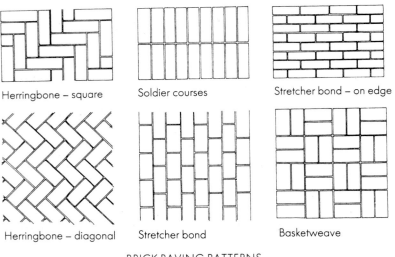

Herringbone – square   Soldier courses   Stretcher bond – on edge

Herringbone – diagonal   Stretcher bond   Basketweave

BRICK PAVING PATTERNS

Stable pavers are just what they say they are. You can get both old and new ones and they have either a diamond pattern or look like a bar of chocolate. Like setts, they are a contrast material and good for drives.

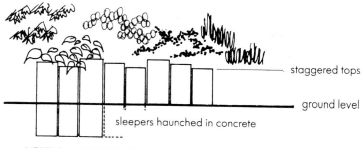

staggered tops

ground level

sleepers haunched in concrete

VERTICAL SLEEPER RETAINING WALL

Timber is a versatile paving material and can be used in a number of ways. Railway sleepers are solid and indestructible, they can be used either as paving, steps, stacked as raised beds or act as a retaining wall. If you are building a bed or retaining wall they should be laid dry and in the same pattern as you would lay bricks. If there are more than three layers it is a good idea to drill and pin them together with reinforcing rod.

Decking is another excellent use of timber and one that should be more widely adopted in this country. Ventilation beneath the surface is essential but decks can be built easily, warm up quickly and look superb. Logs are readily available from storm-damaged trees and slices of large trunks can make ideal informal stepping-stones through a planted area or even attractive seats. Nail chicken wire on the surface of stepping-stones to prevent them becoming slippery.

STEPS

Steps are an essential part of any garden that has a change in level. They should always be as wide and as generous as possible; there is nothing meaner, or more dangerous, than a narrow, steep flight. All the materials just mentioned can be used but match these with surfaces used elsewhere and keep the layout simple. Always ensure that steps are laid to a slight 'fall' so that water drains off them and prevents a freezing death-trap in winter. (See diagram overleaf.)

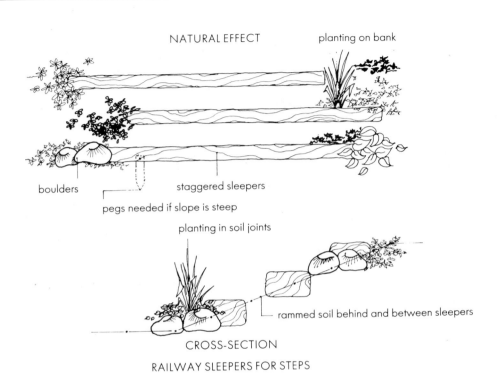

NATURAL EFFECT   planting on bank

boulders

pegs needed if slope is steep

staggered sleepers

planting in soil joints

rammed soil behind and between sleepers

CROSS-SECTION

RAILWAY SLEEPERS FOR STEPS

6

PLANNING: THE DETAILS

FURNITURE

There is a dearth of good garden furniture in this country but it's still really worth shopping around. What you need is something that suits you and suits the design of the garden. Remember that fashion is quite different from good design and there really are some ghastly designs around that people often buy just for the sake of it. Curved iron chairs are one example that look out of place unless you have a period house. (I also find them pretty uncomfortable to sit on!)

Well-made plastic furniture can be ideal, particularly for modern houses. Designed to stand out all year, it is rot proof, it looks good and is undoubtedly comfortable. You can also get cushions and tablecloths that match a scheme inside the house. This type of furniture looks fine in most settings, is easy to clean and unpretentious. If you have a white set, and most are, get a parasol otherwise the glare will nearly blind you, alternatively always use a tablecloth.

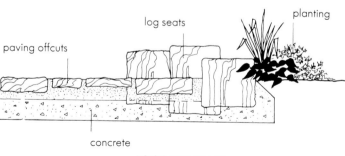

LOGS FOR SEATS

I'm also very fond of deck chairs and those canvas Director chairs, which are comfortable and fold up for easy storage. You can go mad with some gorgeous fabrics!

Timber furniture tends to be rather more sedate, but is perfect for some settings, particularly older, more traditional styles of architecture. Such furniture usually stands out all year and needs regular applications of preservative. A good bench often looks attractive at the end of a path or in an informal sitting area where it has a purpose and acts as a focal point.

Impossibly expensive traditional hardwood seats like those designed by Lutyens have recently made a revival. Lutyens is one of my heroes but he would have had a fit to see how people position faithful replicas of his furniture, often completely out of proportion and clashing with the overall style of the garden. To choose such furniture is often snobbery *par excellence* and the only consolation is that it costs the purchasers a fortune.

Don't always just think of furniture as movable; a raised bed can be designed with a wide wall that doubles as a seat, as can a pool. Seats around trees are also fun as well as practical. Why not build these as a wide platform, perhaps 2.4m (8ft) square; they will double as table, play surface and sunlounger. Upturned logs slightly sunk into the ground are also a good idea. Garden design is all about lateral thinking – keep at it! Hammocks are best of all on a summer's day, although they take a bit of practice to get in and out of. Make sure the fixings are secure.

BARBECUES

Barbecues can either be portable or built into the layout of the patio or sitting area. If the house is brick then echo this in construction, and make sure the cooking area is of ample size for a good party. Built-in seating can be incorporated to one side while overhead beams can help to define the area as well as acting as a frame for a tarpaulin in showery weather! Site a barbecue close to the kitchen for obvious reasons and, if it catches evening sun, then so much the better.

BUILT-IN BARBECUE AND SEAT

I personally still think that wood or charcoal gives the best flavour but some enlightened builders now lay on gas to the garden. Bottled gas or electricity are also possible alternatives.

Simple barbecues can be built from materials to hand, bricks or even concrete blocks laid dry. Sometimes these instant ones are the most successful, as outside eating can often be a spontaneous affair.

PERGOLAS

Pergolas are often a cliché in garden design terms and are sited with little regard to the overall layout and built from unsuitable materials. Any feature like this should be thought about when working on the initial layout, even if it is built at a later stage when time or budget allows.

A pergola should always have somewhere to go and is a marvellous tool for directing the feet or eye in a certain direction, around or across a garden for instance. If the layout is curved it will engender mystery, if straight, can focus the eye on a seat or ornament of some kind. As a screen they are hard to beat, softening a bad view (see page 34) or leading you away from it altogether. They are also the perfect vehicle for climbing plants that can grow where there is ample light and air, as opposed to close to a building where soil can be shallow and rainfall minimal.

Construction should be solid and simple. Stay well-clear of rustic timber which rots quickly and has the worst ring of suburbia about it. Timber posts and beams are fine but if you can run to brick piers, and the garden is big enough to take it visually, so much the better.

WATER FEATURES

When people think of water in the garden they naturally assume that it will take the form of some kind of pool and, in many cases, this is indeed the case. As a general rule, if a pool is situated close to the house, within a crisp paved area, then it should respect the line and pattern of that area. In other words, the shape will usually be rectangular. Further away from the house the shapes of lawns and planted areas may become altogether more fluid and this can be echoed in the design of a pool which can have a more free form shape.

Traditionally, pools of any shape were formed from concrete. This, however, led to problems with hairline cracks that were almost impossible to find. Today the use of plastic and flexible butyl rubber pool liners is more commonplace. These are not only a good deal easier to install, they are also tough and durable. Keep clear of the pastel blue kind, or those that have been printed to simulate pebbles, they are frankly awful and just go a dirty green. Black is by far the best colour for a pool as it tends to reflect the light back and make you unaware of the depth of water. As far as the depth is concerned 45cm (18in) is usually enough in a garden situation, but not much less.

PLANNING: THE DETAILS

When siting a pool make sure that it is in an open sunny position away from overhanging trees. If leaves are a problem then throw a lightweight net over the pool in early autumn, removing it when they have all fallen. For a really healthy pool it is best to have a combination of fish and plants.

Of course, when young children are present, there is a constant fear of an accident. Some of these dangers can be overcome by raising the pool by about 45cm (18in) which will at least act as a deterrent. Another attractive alternative, however, is to construct a 'millstone' feature. This involves either sinking a water tank into the ground or siting one within a raised bed. Two brick piers are built within the tank, the millstone, a drilled piece of slate or even a large boulder is rested on the piers. A pipe is led from a submersible pump, up through the stone. The area surrounding the stone can then be filled with loose cobbles, the tank filled with water and the feature switched on. Water will be pumped up and through the stone and return again to the tank in a continuous cycle. Bear in mind, however, that whenever you use electricity in the garden it must be installed with absolute attention to safety. If in doubt, enrol the help of a qualified electrician.

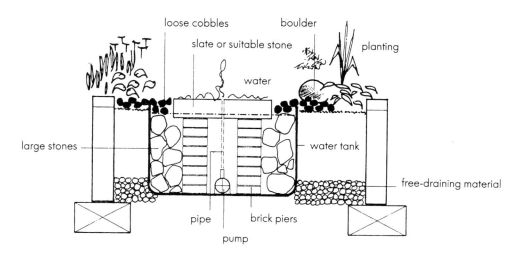

SECTION THROUGH WATER FEATURE

RAISED BEDS

Raised beds are an integral part of any garden, particularly close to the house where they can be easily planned to fit in with the overall pattern of a terrace (see page 33). If the bed is freestanding, within a patio area, then this effect can be achieved by linking it back to the house by courses or a bold panel of brickwork. Planting can be used to soften the appearance of the bed, while the height, if about 45cm (18in), makes the feature an ideal occasional seat. Personally, I see also no point in bending down to tend plants when they can be quite easily raised to a much more comfortable height. Raised beds can also be built against a garden wall where they will naturally help to break up the line, or else used as a device for giving young material a vertical boost, helping to give them an instant air of maturity.

Such beds are also ideal for some of the more rampant plants, and herbs in particular which have an enthusiastic root run. Soil conditions can be varied too – here is an opportunity to grow plants that might not thrive in the soil type of your open garden.

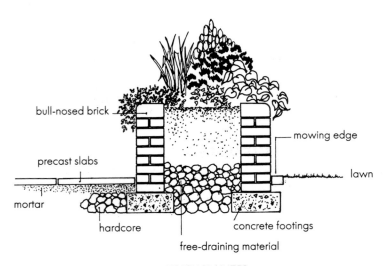

bull-nosed brick

precast slabs

mortar

hardcore

free-draining material

mowing edge

lawn

concrete footings

BRICK PLANTER

CHILDREN'S PLAY AREA

The concept of a 'children's play area' is somewhat meaningless; they quite simply play everywhere and quite rightly so. The criteria for the siting of various pieces of equipment largely depends on age. A toddler, for instance, will need to be in view of one or other parent for much of the time and so a sandpit is best sited close to the house, preferably in the sun, and within a paved area to enable spillage to be swept up easily. A raised pit is good fun and can be converted into a raised bed or pool in later years. Be sure to have a cover for your sandpit that can be fitted in the evening to discourage nocturnal visitors.

Swings and slides are not the most attractive garden features and, if you can allocate space away from the main vista, then so much the better. If they are positioned on the lawn, the grass will quickly be worn away and the area will get very muddy in wet weather. A surface of chipped bark is ideal and makes for soft landings. The area can be contained with boards sunk into the ground just below the level of the surrounding turf.

Wendy houses bought off the peg are usually pretty grim, most dog kennels look better. Kids, however, love to get away into their own 'place' and if you can build a suitable house they will love you for it.

I'm often asked to include a children's growing plot into a design but I rarely do. I know from my own mob that the urge for gardening comes and goes – it's far easier and more practical to let them grow things in the main garden borders. Instant, or near instant results to maintain interest are essential so go for sun flowers, runner beans, annual plants and anything else that is fast-growing and vibrant in colour.

THE UGLY BITS

As I said earlier, the garden has to contain the ugly things as well as the beautiful. In order to make sense of these, group them together. The dustbins, fuel store or oil tank can often be sited in one place, screened by a trellis and rampant climber (one place where Russian vine really is great).

Alternatively, design a neat fence behind which they can be tucked, perhaps extending the line of the house or picking up the style of fencing elsewhere. Sheds, greenhouses, compost bins and incinerators are another generic group and again can be sited close to one another. Not only will this allow multiple screening but it will enable one path to serve the lot, simplifying the garden pattern and rationalising the design. Remember that the greenhouse will need sun and the compost shade, the shed won't care but don't site it so it shades the greenhouse! If possible, create an area of hard standing outside any garden building so you can pause with a barrow or have room to back out with a lawnmower.

CONSERVATORIES

There has been an explosion in conservatories over the last few years and understandably so as they form the perfect link between house and garden, particularly when plants are massed on either side of the glass. Style, however, is important, so buy something that respects the adjoining architecture (see page 35). There is nothing more contrived than a mock-Victorian conservatory tacked onto a mid-thirties semi or, for that matter, a cheap contemporary design stuck on a period house.

The sunny side of the house is the ideal place for a conservatory but try to avoid overhanging trees as fallen leaves can be almost impossible to remove.

SUMMERHOUSES

There is an astonishing array of these freestanding garden buildings but most of them are pretty tacky. A good summerhouse is a genuine focal point (see page 35) and is best used, as the term suggests, in a sunny part of the garden in conjunction with an informal sitting area and preferably linked back to the house by a path. In a small garden they tend to be overpowering and in most situations benefit from a background of planting that will soften their outline. If you are really keen, look through some of the old gardening books that are being reprinted to get ideas, anything by Gertrude Jekyll is a terrific source of fabulous designs.

SPECIAL EFFECTS

Gimmicks are rarely successful in a garden, special effects, however, are a rather different and more considered affair. To work properly any feature like this must genuinely trick you at first sight. Mirrors are perhaps the most successful special effects; a well-positioned mirror, taken right down to ground level in a town garden wall, will instantly create the impression of a way into another area. Angle it slightly so that your reflection is not immediately apparent and wrap it around with plants and you may well get a shock as you try to walk through it!

An old door fixed to a wall is also fun, particularly if it is dressed up with pots on either side and a broad step constructed in front. Some murals too can be stunning and are a feature that take us full circle back to the Roman garden. If these are skilfully painted, a landscape can open up before you in the tiniest yard. Such effects are even better viewed from inside with a pane of glass to slightly blur the trickery.

In a larger garden you can play around with false perspective by narrowing a long pool or paved area as it gets further from a view point. Trees or planting can echo this theory, but the whole effect is decidedly off when looking back the other way! On the whole I leave this alone unless I want something really outrageous. Similarly, I tend to find those false perspective trellis arrangements both a sham and often pretentious.

CONTAINERS

Pots and containers are very much part of the garden furnishings and can be filled with virtually anything you like, from instant annual planting, to shrubs or herbs. They can bring colour to a paved area and can be moved about easily (with castors if the tub is really heavy).

As a general rule, the larger the container the better as this will allow an ample root run and prevent drying out too quickly. Also bear in mind that you can provide a special soil mix for plants that may not be successful in other parts of the garden. Many plants also thrive in the slightly root bound

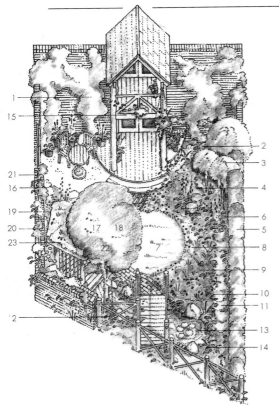

HOUSE WALL
1 *Lonicera periclymenum*
Hedera helix
Lathyrus sylvestris

FERNERY
2 *Asplenium scolopendrium*
3 *Betula pendula*
4 *Digitalis purpura*
Dipsacus fullonum
Silene dioica
Cornus sanguinea
Glechoma hederacea

HEDGEROW
5 *Crataegus monogyna*
Viburnum opulus
Cornus sanguinea
Ilex aquifolium
Euonymus europaeus
Corylus avellana

HEDGE BOTTOM
6 *Alliaria petiolata*
Stellaria holostea
Digitalis purpurea
Stachys sylvatica
7 Traditionally mown lawn
8 Daisy turf

WILD FLOWER MINI MEADOW
9 *Briza media*
Deschampsia flexuosa
Millium effusum 'Aureum'

DITCH BANK
10 *Silene dioica*
Ranunculus acris

DITCH BOTTOM
11 *Ajuga reptans*
Campanula trachelium
Viola riviniana
Primula vulgaris

MARSH PLANTS
12 *Lychnis flos-cuculi*
Cardamine pratensis

DEEP WATER PLANTS
13 *Nymphaea alba*
Ranunculus aquatilis
Veronica beccabunga

SHALLOW WATER PLANTS
14 *Caltha palustris*
Butomus umbellatus
Iris pseudacorus
Carex nigra

WILD FLOWER WINDOW BOX, TUBS AND HANGING BASKETS
15 *Ornithogalum unbellatum*
Aira caryophyllea
Campanula rotundifolia
Anthyllis vulneraria
Viola tricolor
Myosotis arvensis

HERBS
16 *Silene alba*
Thymus drucei
Saponaria officinalis
Oenothera odorata
17 (Behind tree)
Chrysanthemum segetum
Papaver rhoeas
18 (Behind tree)
Leucanthemum vulgare
Vicia sativa
Lotus corniculatus
Verbascum thapsus
Geranium phaeum
Centaurea nigra

TOP OF WALL
19 *Dianthus deltoides*
Thymus drucei
Centranthus ruber
Cheiranthus cheiri

SHADY SIDE OF WALL
20 *Asplenium ruta-muraria*
Geranium robertianum
Hedera helix
Cryptogramma crispa

SUNNY SIDE OF WALL
21 *Cymbalaria muralis*
Teucrium chamaedrys
22 *Quercus robur*

THE WATCH
23 Gazebo with grass/wild flower turf on the roof

'Wildlife, Wild Flower Garden' by Julie Toll
(see page 49).

Above: *The Jones's garden – before (see page 24).*

Right: *A very alternative design for the Jones's garden by Alex Dingwall-Main (see page 101).*

The Jones's garden – after – once it is established (see page 88).

1–2	Specimen shrub with gold foliage, e.g., *Choisya ternata* 'Sundance', *Philadelphus coronarius* 'Aureus'.	
3–8	Lower-growing golden plants, e.g., *Phormium tenax* 'Variegatum'. *Juniperus pfitzerana* 'Aurea'.	
9–13	Variegated shrubs, e.g., *Euonymus fortunei* 'Emerald and Gold', *Lonicera nitida* 'Baggesen's Gold'.	
14–22	Shrubs with blue/mauve foliage and flowers, e.g., *Caryopteris ×* *clandonensis* 'Heavenly Blue', rosemary, *Ceanothus* vars, *Hebe* 'Autumn Glory'.	
23–26	Ground cover in gravel in purples and blues, e.g., *Ajuga reptans* 'Atropurpurea', creeping thyme.	
27 and 44–46	Upright conifers in four sizes, e.g., *Chamaecyparis lawsonia* 'Elwoodii'.	
28, 29	Dense, dark foliage, e.g., *Viburnum tinus* with underplanting, e.g., *Vinca minor*.	
30–33	Dark-foliage wall shrubs, e.g., *Pittosporum*,	

Ceanothus vars plus ground cover, e.g., *Vinca minor*.

64–68	Climbers with dark foliage and flowers, e.g., *Hydrangea petiolaris*.
34–40 and 42	Rich, dense, green foliage, e.g., *Elaeagnus × ebbingei*, *Lonicera pileata*.
41	Silver 'halo' for pool, e.g., *Stachys lanata*.
43	Small specimen tree, e.g., *Pyrus salicifolia* 'Pendula'.
47	Heathers with bronze and golden foliage, e.g., *Calluna* 'Blazeaway', *Erica* 'Foxhollow'.
48–60	Mixed shrubs in 'warm' shades for year-round effect, e.g., *Cornus* 'Westonbirt', *Spiraea* 'Goldmound', *Mahonia* 'Charity', *Cotinus coggyria* 'Royal Purple'.
61–63	Climbers on trellis in shades of yellow and orange, e.g., *Jasminum nudiflorum*, climbing roses 'Albertine', 'Golden Showers'.
69–71	Darker, twining climbers, e.g., *Vitis coignetiae*.

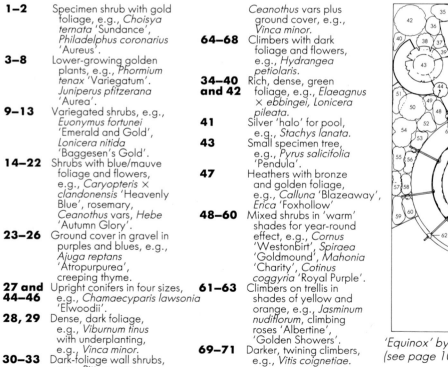

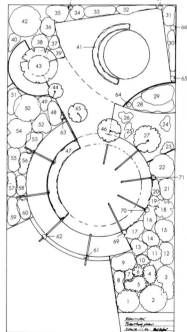

'Equinox' by Paul Cooper (see page 101).

1. 1 *Lonicera japonica* 'Halliana'
2. 4 *Tellima grandiflora* 'Purpurea'
3. 1 *Hedera colchica* 'Dentata Aurea'
4. 3 *Hosta* 'Royal Standard'
5. 1 Clematis – large-flowered, blue/pale mauve
6. 1 *Rosa* 'Maigold'
7. 2 *Vinca major*
8. 1 Heather (existing)
9. 1 *Jasminum nudiflorum*
10. 1 Hebe (existing)
11. 1 *Hebe* 'La Seduisante'
12. 1 *Helianthemum nummularium* 'Wisley Primrose'
13. 1 *Cornus alba* 'Elegantissima'
14. 1 *Garrya elliptica*
15. 1 *Berberis thunbergii* 'Rose Glow'
16. 2 *Salvia officinalis* 'Purpurascens'
17. 2 *Anaphalis triplinervis*
18. 1 *Rosa rubrifolia*
19. 1 *Hedera canariensis* 'Variegata'
20. 1 *Escallonia* 'Edinensis'
21. 1 Pyracantha (existing)
22. 1 *Pyracantha coccinea* 'Mojave'
23. 1 *Euonymus fortunei* 'Emerald Gaiety'
24. 1 *Nandina domestica* 'Firepower'
25. 1 *Rosa* 'Schoolgirl'
26. 3 *Epimedium perralderianum*
27. 1 *Saxifraga umbrosa*
28. 1 *Dianthus* 'Doris'
29. 1 *Campanula alliariifolia* 'Ivory Bells'
30. 2 *Ajuga reptans* 'Atropurpurea'
31. 1 Silver thyme
32. 1 Silver thyme
33. 1 *Choisya ternata*
34. 1 *Helianthemum nummularium* 'Wisley Pink'
35. 3 *Campanula poscharskyana* 'Stella'
36. 1 *Osmanthus burkwoodii*
37. 1 *Lavandula augustifolia* 'Vera'
38. 2 *Aubrieta* – pink
39. 2 *Dianthus* 'Mrs Sinkins'
40. 1 *Hedera helix* 'Glacier'
41. Cotoneaster (existing)
42. 1 *Senecio* 'Sunshine'
43. 1 *Fuchsia magellanica* 'Versicolour'
44. 2 Agapanthus – blue
45. 1 *Lavandula spica*
46. 1 *Clematis* 'Marie Boisselot'
47. 1 *Ceanothus* 'Autumnal Blue'
48. Conifer (existing)
49. 1 *Jasminum officinale*
50. 5 *Bergenia cordifolia* 'Purpurea' interplanted with 5*Holcus mollis* 'Variegatus'
51. 1 *Clematis montana* 'Grandiflora'
52. 3 *Sarcoccocca humilis*
53. 1 *Vitis coignetiae*

'La Source' *by Paul Cooper*
(See page 102).

situations a pot has to offer. I have included a list of plants suitable for containers on page 108.

The container need not be a thing of great beauty; many plants have fine, over-hanging foliage that will hide everything below. I have a collection of hostas in some pretty unlikely pots; an old wash tub, buckets and, best of all, a bath. They enjoy it and frankly the pot becomes incidental.

The complete opposite to this approach is to use a pot of great beauty simply as a piece of sculpture, it will need no planting, simply a special place to go, a turn of a path or the end of a pergola perhaps.

STATUES AND ORNAMENTS

The choice is endless but this is one area where I very rarely get involved with clients – the purchase should always be based on personal choice. Beauty is very much in the eye of the beholder and if a gnome is what turns you on then that's fine as far as I'm concerned. The most important thing about any feature of this kind is that it should have somewhere positive to go and not just be slapped down anywhere. In most gardens, unless the setting

Area of a wildlife garden designed by Ian Smith and Debbie Roberts (see page 103).

1 The gazebo acts as a focal point for the garden and provides shelter and somewhere to sit throughout the year. It is built with oak timbers, flint walling and grey roof tiles, all materials which are indigenous to the area and used in other buildings nearby. The timber decking contrasts nicely with the gravel, cobbles and water-worn boulders around the pools.
2 Heavy railway sleepers embedded in gravel provide ground-surface interest and, as they are made of natural timber, are particularly fitting in a wildlife garden.
3 Water provides visual interest and is essential to attract wildlife to a garden. Native water plants such as yellow flag iris, arrowhead and sedges are grown at the pool margins.
4 The mass of planting surrounding the gazebo area consists entirely of native species which provide shelter and food for all sorts of wildlife and nesting sites for birds. There is a diverse range of trees and shrubs, for example, guelder rose *(Viburnum opulus)* which has berries for birds to feed on, silver birch *(Betula pendula)* and oak *(Quercus robur)* which support a wide range of insects and consequently other animals that feed on those insects, and elder *(Sambucus niger)* and hawthorn *(Crataegus monogyna)* which both produce flowers and fruit attractive to insects and birds.
5 As the area surrounding the gazebo will be heavily used by people a small number of non-native varieties of plants have been included for their aesthetic and horticultural qualities. For example, *Salix purpurea* 'Gracilis', derived from the native purple willow, is a compact and graceful shrub which looks good near water. *Cornus alba* and *C.a.* 'Sibirica' have been planted for their outstanding winter stem colour, and non-native grasses have been situated for their visual appeal, their year-round interest and for the cover and nesting material they provide for birds.

is rigidly formal, statues look at their best tucked into, and softened by, planting (see page 36).

Modern pieces engender sharp disagreement, something that is not only stimulating but which also encourages people to really look at the object and its setting within the overall composition. In other words, it makes them aware of the design whether they like it or not.

Ornaments can also be very simple, a smooth boulder alongside a path, an old column or, as we have already seen, an empty pot. All qualify as ornaments and all will look good in the right position.

SWIMMING POOLS AND TENNIS COURTS

These need a garden of ample size in which to be sited. By the very nature of their size they will be a dominant feature in any composition and will need integrating in a sensible way.

While swimming pools look inviting during a hot summer they look quite the opposite in the depths of winter. For this reason they are often best screened, either behind a contoured bank that utilises the diggings from the pool, or by some form of fence or heavy planting. Pools also tend to be a focus for noise, particularly from children, so this is another reason for keeping them separate from the house and immediate paved area that surrounds it.

The shape of a pool is important and those dreadul kidney-shaped designs are neither easy on the eye nor much good for serious swimming. Rectangular shapes are best for the latter but, if you do want a free form pool, then build up a pattern using a pair of compasses in much the same way as you planned the borders around the lawn (see page 32).

Tennis courts are even larger and more dominant than pools. Planting, both of trees and shrubs, will help to soften the outline and the use of black or brown netting rather than green will also help to blend it into the landscape. If the garden slopes, even slightly, then there will be an enormous amount of earth moving to get the area level. Think very carefully before siting one.

LIGHTING

Lighting falls into two main categories; practical and decorative. The former is concerned with illuminating specific activities, the drive, garage, doors from the house, a barbecue area, steps and paths. The main requisite is that the light should be functional, there is little point in a high level light beam adjoining a flight of steps – it will simply light the top of your head and not your feet. In this situation a fitting can be recessed into the sides of the steps or even into the risers themselves.

Remember, too, that it is the light rather than the fitting that is important; the incongruity of a fine period coach lamp on a contemporary home, mock-Georgian or not, should be obvious. Equally pretentious are the gas Victorian street lamps (or even worse the modern imitations) that normally end up alongside the drive of a stockbroker's house in leafy Surrey. A prime rule of good design is that an object should be fit for its purpose and fit into its surroundings.

Decorative lighting relies even less on the fitting being visible. Here the light itself and the effect is paramount. Lighting can either pinpoint a feature, a pot or statue perhaps, or be more diffused and light an entire area. Low-level lighting can be most effective, particularly within planting. Plants are normally lit from above by natural light and so to see the underside of leaves and branches can create new patterns and textures that are quite different. Keep clear of green, red and orange bulbs, however, as they turn foliage a sickly hue. White and blue light is fine.

The most exciting developments are taking place with the use of fibre optics, lasers and holograms. Here patterns can be woven of an entirely different kind; stabbing shafts, twisting shapes and gently diffused streamers of colour can be interwoven in an ever-changing pattern. All of these can be linked into a synthesizer and open up an entirely new dimension that allows the garden to be used for 24-hours-a-day.

7

PLANTING

To most people it is the plants that are a garden. I have tried to demonstrate, however, that the hard landscape structure is also extremely important, not only to provide all those features that bring the 'living room' to life in practical terms, but also to act as a frame whose outline will be softened by the plants it supports.

Unfortunately it is still true that the whole subject of plants and planting tends to be surrounded with mystery, all those confusing Latin names and even the simple fact that plants grow to proportions far beyond the small pot they arrived in! Don't, as we said earlier, rush out to the nearest garden centre and impulse-buy the first plants that catch your fancy, the odds are that they will be quite wrong. Like planning the basic design of the garden, your planting scheme also needs to be worked out in a logical sequence. It is well worth while doing some basic homework. Read good plant books, visit gardens, jot down names of what you fancy and take a photograph to remind yourself what it looks like. Chat to friends, be nosey over the garden wall – gardeners and plants-people are usually happy to talk and only too keen to offer advice.

A LESSON FROM NATURE

If you go into a woodland you will see plants growing in a natural environment. In many areas you will see a top canopy of trees below which is growing a shrubby layer of lower plants. Beneath this there will probably be a dense ground cover of bramble, ivy or even perhaps honeysuckle. All these layers co-exist in harmony, each doing a different job and thriving in different conditions. There is little maintenance in a well-balanced woodland!

In the garden it will make sense to copy this basic pattern, albeit with more decorative species that will provide colour and interest throughout the year (see page 37).

BUILDING UP A FRAMEWORK

When we carried out our basic garden survey we identified certain problem areas. The direction of a prevailing wind, a bad view or a neighbour's garage that needed screening. To provide such shelter and screening we will need to plan a background of tough, largely evergreen planting that can act as a barrier and provide a backdrop for the lighter more colourful material that can be used in the foreground. Most of these plants need to be relatively fast growers: bamboo, elaeagnus, laurel, viburnum, berberis, choisya and photinia are just a few suitable species. There is a more detailed list of plants that are suitable for screening on page 105.

One of the great mistakes in many gardens is that shrubs get planted in isolation which tends to lead to a jumble of unrelated species. Even the largest shrubs look far better planted as a group rather than a single specimen and this also helps to give the general composition of the garden far greater continuity.

Trees are of course an integral part of this 'framework' planting. They are also an important element of the overall design, providing different emphasis according to the shape and helping to balance one feature with another. For this reason it is vital to know what shape a tree will be when it is mature.

Choose trees carefully bearing in mind the size of the garden. In a small area, forest trees such as oak, ash, sycamore, and particularly willow and

DIFFERENT SHAPES OF TREES

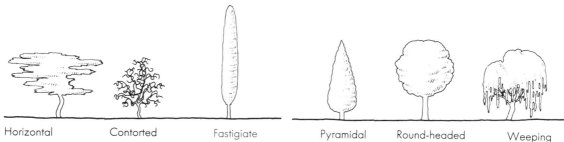

Horizontal
e.g. *Picea pungens*

Contorted
e.g. *Corylus contorta*

Fastigiate
e.g. *Prunus* 'Amanogawa'

Pyramidal
e.g. bay tree

Round-headed
e.g. *Malus* species

Weeping
e.g. willow

poplar, would be totally out of scale, but birch, rowan and eucalyptus, for instance, would all be fine.

The dividing line between screening plants that form the framework of the garden and lower growing, more decorative material, is not clear cut and nor should it be. The two elements should mix together to form an ever-changing pattern throughout the year. Flowers will play a greater role in the middle and front of the border while the leaf shape and texture will be an important element throughout.

COLOUR SCHEMES

Colour is a vital ingredient in any garden but it is fair to say that there is very little that is entirely new in any area of design and that also includes outside decoration. Even so, it is always worth getting inspiration from the experts (see page 38).

In this country it was that great plants-lady, Gertrude Jekyll, who really put the theory of colour into reasonable perspective during the first part of this century. She was a painter who turned to gardening when her eyesight began to fail. She said, in very simplistic terms, that the hot colours such as red, orange and yellow, tend to draw the eye and should therefore be used close to the house or main view point of a garden, and that the cooler colours, including blues, pink, purple and pastels, should be used further away and thus increase the feeling of distance and space.

You can easily prove this by placing a tub full of bright red tulips or pelargoniums at the bottom of the lawn. Your eye immediately jumps down to it and foreshortens the garden in the process, you simply don't bother to look at the less vibrant colours, however attractive they may be. Grey, as in most areas of design, is a great harmoniser. You can use it to link and tie colour ranges together, as well to tone down any excesses!

TEXTURE AND FORM

Many plants have handsome foliage, some with leathery leaves, some with bright variegation, some veined, some glossy and so on. When planted in groups and drifts these can set up a fascinating dialogue as can the colour of a stem or the shape of one plant against the next.

Rounded forms look good next to a spiky or fastigiate shape. Prostrate or sprawling plants enhance the line of a retaining wall, raised bed or sculptural group of smooth boulders. They also associate harmoniously with species that grow vertically.

Conifers need particular mention as these are the punctuation marks of any scheme. The upright varieties draw the eye and should be used carefully to emphasise or bring interest to a particular area. Too many in a garden, however, are visually unsettling as the eye jumps all over the place in an effort to see them all. If you like conifers, and there is no doubt that they have a stunning variety of form and foliage, then I suggest you grow them as a collection so that you can see the beauty of one against another in a controlled setting.

INSTANT GARDENS

There is no such thing as an instant garden, even those at the Chelsea Flower Show take time to build and are so densely planted that they would be a riot after a few months' growth! However, certain gardens can mature faster than others and this is largely down to the choice of plant material and the density in which it is planted. The average well-designed plot should reach a reasonable state of maturity in 3–5 years. To achieve this you want to plant a combination of faster growing shrubs, such as buddleia, broom and mallow, in amongst your slower developers. Most fast-growers can be cut back hard each year and can, if necessary, be removed altogether once the slower material has started to knit together.

Herbaceous or hardy perennial plants are marvellous fillers in a border and reach maturity in two or three seasons. In my own garden I have used masses of them, including hostas, alchemilla, rheum, geraniums, sedums and so on. You can be quite firm with them, lifting and dividing them every three years or so, as necessary. I must admit though, I just let mine run on and only take a spade to them if things get totally out of control.

GARDENS BY DESIGN

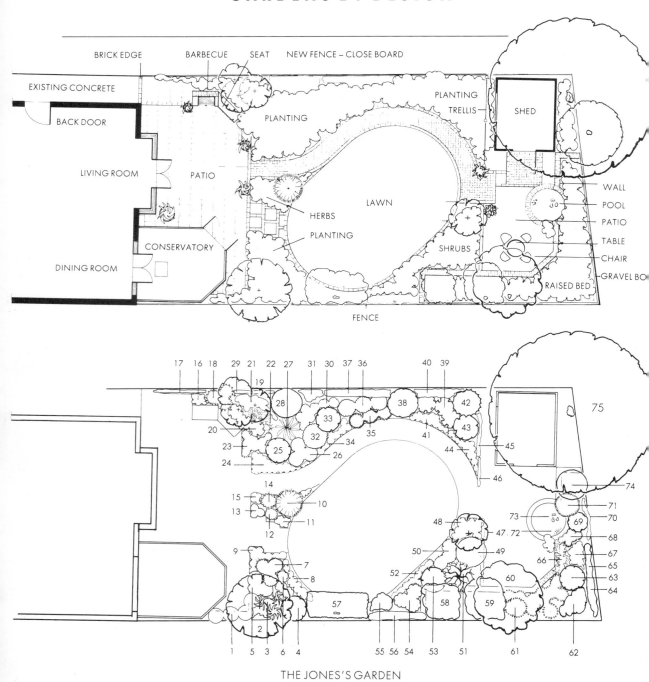

BRICK EDGE   BARBECUE   SEAT   NEW FENCE – CLOSE BOARD

EXISTING CONCRETE

BACK DOOR

PLANTING

PLANTING

TRELLIS

SHED

LIVING ROOM

PATIO

HERBS

LAWN

WALL

POOL

PATIO

PLANTING

TABLE

SHRUBS

CHAIR

CONSERVATORY

DINING ROOM

GRAVEL BO

RAISED BED

FENCE

THE JONES'S GARDEN

YEAR-ROUND INTEREST

There are two prime rules in planting design; one says that you should never be a slave to a garden, the other that you should have colour and interest throughout the year. Both of these rely on your ability to do that essential homework or, alternatively, to enrol the help of a designer who can work out the right plants for the right place. A sensible approach might be for you to carry out the basic design of the garden and then call in a professional to do the planting layout for you. In this way you get the best of both worlds, your ideas on how the space should work, and their specialised knowledge of how to bring it to life.

Whichever approach you take it is always worth jotting down your favourite plants so that these can be worked into the composition. Try and get a mixture of these, some trees, some shrubs, herbaceous, annuals and

1 4 Euonymus fortunei 'Emerald and Gold'
2 1 Gleditsia triacanthos 'Sunburst'
3 3 Phormium tenax 'Yellow Wave'
4 1 Mahonia japonica
5 3 Euphorbia robbiae (existing)
6 3 Hemerocallis 'Golden Chimes'
7 3 Salvia officinalis 'Icterina'
8 9 Alyssum saxatilis 'Compactum'
9 9 Thymus × citriodorus 'Aureus'
10 1 Rosmarinus officinalis
11 7 Petroselinum crispum
12 1 Lavandula angustifolia 'Vera'
13 3 Thymus drucei
14 1 Salvia officinalis
15 3 Allium schoenoprasum
16 3 Vinca minor 'Aureovariegata'
17 1 Rosa 'Zéphirine Drouhin'
18 3 Phalaris arundinacea picta
19 1 Betula pendula 'Dalecarlica'
       1 Betula pendula 'Purpurea'
       1 Betula davurica
20 3 Polystichum setiferum
21 7 Digitalis purpurea
22 3 Hosta 'Royal Standard'
23 8 Hosta undulata 'Medio-variegata'
24 10 Helianthemum nummularium 'Wisley Pink'
25 1 Buxus sempervirens
26 3 Euonymus fortunei 'Emerald Gaiety'

27 1 Hebe salicifolia
28 1 Osmanthus burkwoodii
29 2 Hedera helix 'Green Ripple'
30 7 Sidalcea malviflora 'Mrs Alderson'
31 1 Clematis 'Madame Le Coultre'
32 1 Rosa 'The Fairy'
33 1 Hebe anomala
34 8 Veronica teucrium 'Shirley Blue'
35 3 Santolina chamaecyparissus
36 3 Caryopteris incana × mongolica 'Kew Blue'
37 1 Vitis vinifera (existing)
38 1 Choisya ternata
39 3 Weigela florida 'Aureovariegata'
40 1 Lonicera japonica 'Halliana (existing)
41 7 Salvia 'Rose Queen'
42 1 Ilex aquifolium 'J. C. Van Tol'
43 1 Hebe 'Midsummer Beauty' (existing)
44 11 Campanula portenschlagiana
45 1 Hedera colchica 'Dentata Variegata'
46 1 Rosa 'Compassion'
47 1 Family apple tree
48 9 Prunella grandiflora webbiana 'Loveliness Pink' (existing)
49 1 Skimmia japonica
50 3 Cistus 'Sunset'
51 1 Viburnum × burkwoodii
52 10 Festuca glauca
53 1 Hebe 'Great Orme'
54 3 Hydrangea serrata 'Preziosa' (existing)

55 1 Chaenomeles × superba 'Crimson and Gold' (existing)
56 1 Lonicera periclymenum 'Serotina' (existing)
57 1 Viburnum tinus (existing)
58 1 Berberis thunbergii 'Atropurpurea' (existing)
59 1 Escallonia × langleyensis 'Apple Blossom' (existing)
60 1 Pyracantha coccinea 'Orange Charmer' (existing)
61 9 Azaleas mixed Japanese species (existing)
62 1 Hedera helix (existing on tree stump)
63 1 Pieris formosa forrestii (existing)
64 1 Actinidia kolomikta
65 1 Jasminum officinale
66 1 Hedera helix 'Eva'
67 7 Penstemon × gloxinioides 'Firebird'
68 7 Molinia caerulea 'Variegata'
69 1 Philadelphus 'Manteau d'Hermine'
70 1 Rosa 'Guinée'
71 1 Juniperus horizontalis 'Emerald Spreader' (existing)
72 1 Iris laevigata 'Rose Queen'
73 1 Nymphaea pygmaea 'Alba'
74 1 Fatsia japonica
75 1 Crataegus oxyacantha (existing)

so on. You might get a few ideas from the Jones's garden (designed for the television series), see page 88.

MAINTENANCE

The common perception of plants is that the more you have the greater the work in looking after them. In fact it is quite the other way about. If you have a few shrubs and hardy perennials dotted about a border with a sea of soil in between, it is pretty obvious that you are going to spend a good deal of time in keeping the area clear of weeds. If, on the other hand, you structure your planting scheme in the way we have suggested, with a top storey of trees, a shrubby middle layer and then a carpet of low-growing ground-covering plants, then maintenance can be reduced to a very low level.

Certain features need more maintenance than others. A rockery or series of well-positioned rock outcrops tend to involve a relatively high level of maintenance as those pockets of soil can be quickly colonised by weeds rather than alpines. On the other side of the coin, an area given over to rougher grass, naturalised with bulbs and wild flowers can be a delight throughout the year with very little to do except three or four cuts with a rotary mower. All-in-all very good value indeed.

It would be wrong, however, to think that a complete carpet of plants eliminates maintenance altogether. You may well have to cut back invasive ground cover from time to time, as well as thinning out a border if it becomes overcrowded. These jobs, however, consume relatively little time and in my own garden, which is of a reasonable size, I spend a maximum of half-an-hour a week on maintenance – and I enjoy it!

Finally, give a thought to automatic irrigation. A hot summer can bring home just how important regular watering really is, particularly if you go away on holiday. There are a number of low-cost irrigation systems available that are tailor-made for the domestic garden and it could be well-worth investigating these. Incidentally, they also use far less water than a sprinkler and are positioned so that planting gets the maximum benefit.

MY OWN BACK GARDEN

At home I very much try to practise what I preach and have designed a garden that we use a great deal, for a wide range of activities. It is essentially a long narrow plot at the rear of an Edwardian house, the length is approximately 90m (300ft), the width just 8m (25ft). The ground slopes gently away from the house, the soil is just on the acid side of neutral and the whole area faces due south. All of these are factors that made us buy the property in the first place!

Next to the house I have provided ample room for sitting and dining, using a combination of old blue stable pavers and neat precast slabs (see page 40). In order to increase the feeling of width I have used 60cm×30cm (2ft×1ft) precast concrete slabs, laid in a stretcher bond across the space. Raised beds bring planting up to a workable height and I have built in a dustbin store and barbecue close to the back door and kitchen. A raised pool has been positioned to one side of the terrace, this having a decorative mask and spout that adds a little movement and sound to the area. A wall just over 1m (3¼ft) high divides this 'room' from the next with broad steps linking the two levels. From here a path leads down one side of the lawn (set just below the grass to allow easy mowing) and turns through 90° just in front of a mature conifer. This area is essentially given over to grass and play, we use a tennis trainer in the summer, the dogs lie around, and the whole composition is wrapped around with planting.

Even broader steps drop down to the third room which I am encouraging to go wild. It is dominated by two old lilacs and a sumach. The latter is sending up suckers all over the place and usually I just let them go, only removing them if they start to overhang the stepping stone path and become a nuisance. There are some old raspberry canes here, too, which have gone wild and I have also planted drifts of ground cover that include pulmonaria and *Geranium endressii*. I tend to just bung things in this part of the garden; Silver birches, a developing Norway Maple *(Acer platanoides)* – it will be too big eventually – a fatshedera on one of the fences and all sorts of other

MY OWN BACK GARDEN

FENCE

GATE

STEPPING-STONES
THROUGH GROUND
COVER

STEPS

COLUMN AND BUST

LAWN

MIXED PLANTING

MIXED PLANTING
WALL
STATUE
OLD STABLE PAVERS

STEPS

WALL

PRECAST SLABS

RAISED POOL
AND SPOUT
RAISED BED

RAISED BED

SEAT
GATE

BARBECUE

SINK

OLD STABLE PAVERS

STORE

DOOR

WINDOW

43

44

42

45

46

41

40

39
38

37

36

35

34

33

32

55   56

31

30

29
28
27

26   61

25

24

23

22

1

2

3

4

5

6

47

7

49   50

48

8

51

9

52

10

60

11

53   54

12

13

14

59

57

15

58

16

17

18

19

20

21

things that have come off the end of landscaping jobs. It is a lovely place, easy to keep under control with the occasional use of a spade, and it even has nettles to attract butterflies.

The last room is the sensible utility area, divided from the former by a well-detailed, slatted, diagonal fence. Here we have got the chickens (great manure once it has calmed down), sheds, bonfire, hardcore tip, some old apple trees, and an area to heel in plants that I have not yet found a home for. It is generally pretty messy, but you need a space like this somewhere.

Our garden is very much a working place, somewhere where we can relax, mess around, grow things or eat, as the mood takes us. It's not perfect, but then I don't trust people that have immaculate gardens, there is something wrong! It's also in a state of flux. This winter an old wall fell down and demolished an entire border, taking with it a fine old established ivy. I'm still uncertain what to do here, but time will tell, and that's what a lot of good design is all about. Don't rush out and do the first thing that comes into your head! Another absolutely essential rule when designing is to relax; laid back gardening works every time for me!

1 1 *Rhododendron yakushimanum* hybrid	**22** 1 *Fatshedera*	**42** 4 *Rhus typhina*
2 2 *Astilbe taquetii superba* 'Glow'	**23** 1 *Rhododendron yakushimanum* hybrid	**43** 2 *Syringa vulgaris*
3 15 *Pulmonaria saccharata*	**24** 3 *Dicentra spectabilis*	**44** 10 *Geranium endressii*
4 12 *Geranium endressii*	**25** 3 *Hosta fortunei* 'Aureomarginata'	**45** 6 *Pulmonaria saccharata*
5 1 *Berberis × stenophylla*	**26** 1 *Parthenocissus henryana*	**46** 2 *Cornus alba* 'Sibirica'
6 1 *Viburnum tinus*	**27** *Ilex aquifolium* (tree)	**47** 2 *Euphorbia griffithii* 'Fireglow'
7 Existing large conifer	**28** 4 *Anemone japonica* (White)	**48** 1 *Phormium cookianum*
8 1 *Elaeagnus × ebbingei*	**29** 3 *Aquilegia* 'Langdon's Strain'	**49** 1 *Cedrus deodara* 'Golden Horizon'
9 1 *Ceanothus* 'Autumnal Blue'	**30** 8 *Alchemilla mollis*	**50** 3 *Hosta sieboldiana*
10 2 *Buddleia davidii* 'Empire Blue'	**31** 4 *Euphorbia polychroma*	**51** 2 *Juniperus scopulorum* 'Skyrocket'
11 Ivy-covered tree stump	**32** 1 *Arundinaria nitida*	**52** 7 *Heuchera* 'Palace Purple'
12 5 *Helleborus foetidissimus*	**33** 1 *Weigela* 'Bristol Ruby'	**53** 3 *Acanthus spinosus*
13 1 *Spiraea × arguta*	**34** 1 *Berberis thunbergii* 'Atropurpurea'	**54** 1 *Passiflora caerulea*
14 1 *Rheum palmatum*	**35** 3 *Senecio greyii*	**55** 2 *Arundinaria viridistriata*
15 3 *Ligularia przewalskii* 'The Rocket'	**36** 1 *Rosa* 'Canary Bird'	**56** 1 *Euonymus fortunei* 'Emerald and Gold'
16 3 *Hosta sieboldiana*	**37** 5 *Sedum* 'Autumn Joy'	**57** 4 *Astilbe* 'Fanal'
17 1 *Hosta fortunei* 'Albopicta'	**38** 3 Hollyhock	**58** 6 *Geranium* 'Russell Prichard'
18 1 *Hebe rakaiensis*	**39** 6 *Geranium* 'Johnson's Blue'	**59** 1 *Helleborus corsicus*
19 2 *Hosta* 'Thomas Hogg'	**40** 3 *Rhododendron yakushimanum* hybrid	**60** 15 *Anemone japonica* (Pink)
20 1 *Actinidia kolomikta*	**41** 1 *Euphorbia wulfenii*	**61** 1 *Euphorbia griffithii* 'Fireglow'
21 Sink for alpines		

8

FRONT GARDENS

While we often lavish a great deal of time, money and planning on the back garden it is a great pity that the area at the front is so often forgotten. It is true that very often the distance between house and street is minimal but this makes it even more important to plan the space properly. Where a back garden is primarily for leisure, the front is geared up for access – for people, cars and delivery vehicles. In short, the pace of life is going to be a good deal quicker in the front garden than it is in the back and so the choice of materials and the way that they are positioned will be of paramount importance.

There is usually a need for ample parking and one of the most difficult problems is how to relate this to the rest of the garden. Very often a drive and the associated parking will be the largest single element and, as such, you should try to use materials that blend well with your house. Good combinations are brick paving and 'brushed' concrete or tarmac and gravel, which can easily be cast or laid to a curve, often an essential part of a front garden layout.

In many small front gardens you often see a separate path to the front door as well as the drive. This tends to chop the space up unnecessarily, it can be far better for the drive to incorporate pedestrian access as well. This being the case, bear in mind that cars tend to take up a lot of room so allow room for both doors to open and for people to get by without being forced onto adjoining planting or a wet lawn.

The focus of a front garden is, of course, the front door so both feet and eye should be led in that direction by a well-worked paving pattern that is reinforced by planting and perhaps raised beds.

PLANTING

Paving and hard landscaping will almost certainly predominate in a front garden thus making whatever planting there is of particular importance to soften and also provide three-dimensional balance to the composition. Unfortunately, pollution is increasingly becoming a problem where gardens adjoin a main road; fumes, noise and a bad view will all impinge on the senses. There are, however, many tough evergreen plants (listed on page 109) that are particularly resistant and it is surprising how much sound a dense border can absorb, particularly if there is room to create a contoured mound along the boundary. A thick hedge is also an excellent screen and one should not forget that any trees you plant will not just be a valuable contribution to your own garden but to the appearance of the street in general. It is true to say that plants in a front garden should have quite different characteristics from those in the back; a softly planted border may engender relaxation in the rear garden but the opposite effect is probably needed in the front. Here you might think of using more strongly shaped species such as yucca, acanthus, phormium or mahonia. Lower-growing ground cover will also be particularly important not just to reduce maintenance but also to spill over and soften the harder lines of the paving. As well as soaking up a deal of noise a background of tougher planting may also discourage short cuts by casual callers or delivery men. Prickly plants do this best of all; berberis, holly and pyracantha are excellent in this respect. Do remember, though, that any hedge or planting should not encroach onto the pavement so keep it regulary clipped back. A well-placed boulder on the corner of a bed will also be an excellent deterrent against short cuts, being a good deal more effective than a battered begonia and more handsome into the bargain.

POTS AND WINDOW BOXES

Front gardens are ideal for these and here you can be as bold with colour as you like. The activity and vibrancy of a street will welcome the brightness of red, yellow and orange flowers. Planting can be either seasonal, which will mean changing it every so often, or permanent with a selection of shrubs to give colour and interest throughout the year.

If you are using window boxes make sure they are secure, particularly if they are outside an upstairs window overhanging the street. Pots will need to be big and heavy otherwise they will be stolen and remember that any containers close to a building may need regular watering as overhanging eaves could prevent rain reaching the roots.

MY OWN FRONT GARDEN

In my own front garden (see page 40) I have done a lot of the things we have just been talking about. The area is in fact tiny and although there might be room for a car at a pinch I'd rather keep the space clear and create a visually more acceptable impression.

I have concentrated on a sensible paving pattern of neat precast slabs with brick to highlight the way to the front door. I have also increased the visual width of what is a very narrow space by running the whole pattern off into an area of planting to one side.

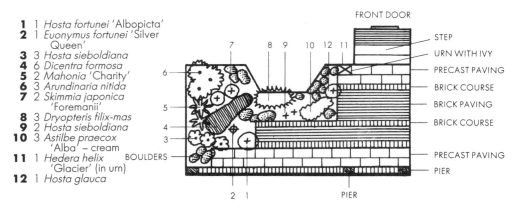

1 1 *Hosta fortunei* 'Albopicta'
2 1 *Euonymus fortunei* 'Silver Queen'
3 3 *Hosta sieboldiana*
4 6 *Dicentra formosa*
5 2 *Mahonia* 'Charity'
6 3 *Arundinaria nitida*
7 2 *Skimmia japonica* 'Foremanii'
8 3 *Dryopteris filix-mas*
9 2 *Hosta sieboldiana*
10 3 *Astilbe praecox* 'Alba' – cream
11 1 *Hedera helix* 'Glacier' (in urn)
12 1 *Hosta glauca*

FRONT DOOR
STEP
URN WITH IVY
PRECAST PAVING
BRICK COURSE
BRICK PAVING
BRICK COURSE
PRECAST PAVING
PIER
BOULDERS
PIER

FRONT GARDENS

The area is far too small for a lawn and so planting occupies the rest of the space. As the garden faces almost due north it stays in shade for most of the day. For that reason I have chosen a pale Cotswold colour precast concrete slab and this reflects as much available light as possible. I have also chosen plants that will thrive in such conditions: bamboo, mahonia, skimmia, hosta, dicentra and astilbe are all ideal here, having bold foliage and delightful flowers at different times of the year. I have also used a good quantity of loose cobbles and boulders to keep passing feet off the planting. These act as sculpture in their own right and provide an excellent ground cover that needs no maintenance at all.

9

ROOF AND BALCONY GARDENS

Roofs do not make ideal gardens. They are either too cold or too hot, depending on the season, and are more often than not racked by high winds. Add to this a variety of structural problems that can range from a weak floor (the ceiling of the room below!), a lack of drainage, and often almost impossible access, and your enthusiasm may wither the first time you stick your head out of a skylight after climbing a flight of rickety stairs!

On the other hand, however, if this is your only open space in a totally urban environment, a combination of determination, imagination, hard work and money can transform this alien world into an oasis; a good rooftop garden can be nothing short of magic (see page 39).

The first consideration in any roof garden should always be safety, both of the underlying structure and the boundaries to the roof itself. If you have any doubts in this area enlist the services of a qualified surveyor or structural engineer. Their fee will be more than worth it and you will be able to sleep easy at night without the fear of half-a-ton of wet compost arriving unexpectedly on your duvet. Whatever the structural strength of the roof, lightweight materials should be used wherever possible. Beds, for example, can normally be constructed from timber rather than bricks or concrete blocks. Not only does this prevent overloading on the roof but also, remember that *all* the materials will need to be brought up from ground level and will doubtlessly seem to get heavier as you climb! For the same reason lightweight compost is also probably a far better bet than garden soil, but it does dry out more quickly and will also need regular feeding to maintain fertility.

It is probably more sensible to have raised beds in your roof garden than pots which will dry out rapidly in this windswept position and also tend to blow over if the plant in them is of a reasonable height. If you do use containers, and chimney pots are a delightful choice, make sure they are as

98

large as possible and *never* stand them on a ledge or parapet where there is a danger of them falling off into the garden or street below.

If shelter is necessary in your roof garden, and it often is, try to use a permeable slatted screen that filters and breaks the speed of the wind. This will create less turbulence than a solid fence or wall. Glass screens are an obvious choice where the view is spectacular but make sure you use the toughened plate type and fix it very firmly in position.

Conventional paving slabs are usually too heavy for a roof, instead, lightweight tiles are often a sensible choice. I'm not at all worried about using imitation grass, it looks fine, does not rot and can be cut into any shape you like, including sweeping curves. Enhance these shapes further with equally bold drifts of coloured gravels to create a surreal picture that echoes the shape and swirl of passing clouds.

Decking is another good choice for a roof garden, being light, easy to construct and simple to fit. It could also pick up the style of slats used for raised beds elsewhere in the garden and, additionally, won't obstruct the drainage beneath. Think also about the colour you paint timber; white is a glaring disaster on a roof as it is far too bright. Cream is fine but a pale stain is probably best of all and relatively easy to maintain. Don't necessarily just think of brown; stains come in a variety of fabulous colours from the palest pastels to the most vibrant primaries. Use them to pick up the colour of blinds, awnings or chair cushions.

Planting is the last job and here you will need to choose real sun lovers and species that are tolerant of high temperatures (select plants from the appropriate lists on page 107). Yucca, senecio, cistus, hebe, potentilla, broom, phlomis and many others will be fine. Do your homework just as you did for the garden at ground level, there are plenty to choose from.

Finally, automatic irrigation could be a real boon in a roof garden and it might be well-worth getting a system installed, particularly if you are away a lot. In any event try and get an outside tap and, of course, install electricity for evening lighting.

10

INSPIRATIONAL STYLES

A good garden designer, more often than not, works from a well-tried and tested set of rules that he or she knows will work under most circumstances. Most designers have a distinctive style and their work can be recognised in exactly the same way as an artist's or sculptor's can. The amateur designer obviously lacks the training of a professional but there is still absolutely no reason why anyone at all cannot produce a sensible and attractive scheme that fits their own requirements exactly, particularly if they go through the design processes that we have talked about in this book.

When it comes to inspiration, however, the amateur designer must remember that this is something that can never be learnt or copied exactly. Inspiration is unique – to try to duplicate another designer's garden will only lead to disaster, no matter how beautiful or well-designed it may be. The reason for this is, of course, that the original was prepared with a particular brief in mind, a specific set of circumstances and requirements which inevitably won't be precisely the same as yours. A Japanese garden can never be reproduced exactly in this country, although certain features of the style, whether in planting or design, can be. For example, you may be able to look at the positioning and textures of rocks in a Japanese garden and reproduce that relationship using different materials. In other words, it is the design *principle* that is important. The principle can be repeated but not the exact subject.

Having said all this there are many styles and designers whose work is emulated, and rightly so. One has only to look at the superb gardens of Sir Edwin Lutyens built during the first part of this century: these are, on the whole, enormous, but his clarity of line, choice of materials and juxtaposition of features, represent design of the highest order. Lutyens also worked successfully with another designer, the great plants-lady, Gertrude Jekyll, and it was her subtle use of form, flower and foliage that breathed life into his stunningly controlled patterns.

Once you start to understand just how such designs work you are well on the way to being a good designer yourself. It doesn't matter that your garden is only a fraction of the size of those that the great designers like Lutyens worked on.

The gardens at Sissinghurst in Kent represent another school of design. Here, hedges and walls separate areas into rooms with the joy of a different type of planting in each. Hidcote Manor in Gloucestershire also echoes these principles.

Other great sources of inspiration are the National Garden Festivals and the Chelsea Flower Show which have a wealth of different gardens and styles, some of which are brilliant and some frankly awful.

Wherever you visit, whether just a friend's garden or a garden belonging to The National Gardens Scheme (see page 110 for details), the trick is to identify the features that you like and then adapt them to suit your own garden.

Some designers are intentionally outrageous; Alex Dingwall-Main, who created the alternative design for the Jones's garden in the television series, is one such designer. It is fascinating to compare his vision of the Jones's garden on pages 74–5 with Julie Toll's on pages 76–7. The work of Paul Cooper is also both stimulating and wonderfully funny, although behind it there still lies an enormous strength of purpose which is why his gardens work so well. He is quite right to be exploring the possibilities of using unlikely materials and colours in his compositions for only by doing this can any designer move forward, develop new ideas and see just how they work in practice. Here are two of Paul's gardens.

'EQUINOX' BY PAUL COOPER (page 78)
Traditionally 20 March is a special day in the garden, it is the vernal equinox and the beginning of spring. It is also the time of equal day and equal night.

'Equinox' is a garden that is designed so that it appears to be lit simultaneously by both the light of the setting sun and of the rising moon.

At one end of the garden is the moon pool patio, encircled by conifers creating a cool blue light, the area is one of stillness and calm. Just a few steps away, and in vivid contrast, is the sunset patio with its radiating 'woodhenge' pergola and fiery array of planting.

'Equinox' is a garden design that creates atmosphere and mystery yet allows enough space for entertainment, play and relaxation.

'LA SOURCE' BY PAUL COOPER (page 79)

An ideal design for a very small garden, the starting point is a trellis feature which creates a two-dimensional 'reverse topiary' of 'La Source'. The idea is taken from a painting by Ingres of a woman pouring water from a pitcher. The water in the garden, however, is suggested rather than actual. The 'splash' as it falls is represented by planting which tumbles over pebbles. The 'water' then re-emerges as a 'stream', an effect which is created by using slate turned on its edge which curls across and divides the garden. There are stepping-stones across and a handrail for balance.

A pergola can also be fixed to the house and thus helps to extend the dining room space into the garden. The pergola is not visible in the elevation of the garden but can be seen in the planting plan.

One of the major problems for any art form is in overcoming our preconceived ideas so we forget our often limited terms of reference. It is vital to be able to do this and to open your mind to other possibilities which just might be a whole lot more exciting.

Remember that ultimately, to use modern jargon, a well-designed garden should 'turn you on' and that, at the end of the day, is what it is all about. If you can adapt an inspirational design in a way that suits you then we have achieved what we set out to do and you are on your way to being a good designer.

11

HOW TO BECOME A
GARDEN DESIGNER

One of the strengths and the weaknesses of garden design is the fact that you need no formal qualifications to do it. Having said that, the number of untrained people who produce work of real merit is very few. Training itself is a contentious subject. Does a lifetime spent working in a nursery or on your own plot count as training? For some it will do, but those people are likely to be outstanding designers anyway, regardless of any formal training.

For most of us study is essential to simply realise our full potential. There are two main methods of becoming a garden designer, the first of which involves training to be a landscape architect. This usually takes the form of a degree course at a university or a polytechnic. It covers not just gardens but the whole spectrum of landscape design and architecture. It is an extremely comprehensive training and many people feel that they would never use all that they had learnt in simply designing gardens. In part they are right, but such a qualification allows you enough scope to pursue a career which has enormous variety, ranging from the landscaping of enormous development projects right down to the design of intimate courtyards. Details of such courses can be obtained from The Landscape Institute. Debbie Roberts and Ian Smith, two young designers who have recently completed such a training, are already designing an extensive wildlife garden for the staff of a large company. A section of their design can be seen on page 80.

For straight garden design there are an increasing number of courses, some part-time and some full-time, which can be as simple or as high-powered as you like. The Society of Landscape and Garden Designers can send you a list of recommended schools. Other courses, which can be of variable quality, are often advertised in *The Garden*, the journal of the Royal

Horticultural Society. Whatever course you choose, go and check it out first. There should be an open evening or a similar opportunity to go and talk to the tutors and assess if it is the right one for you. Try and establish just what they offer and just what you want from the course. Most will give you some kind of diploma but it is fair to say that this only indicates study up to a certain level – the real work of a career starts after that!

At the end of the day, garden design offers one of the most rewarding and fascinating careers and, although you will rarely make a fortune, you will live a rich life, create environments of beauty and practicality and, most importantly, achieve great satisfaction. Good luck!

PLANTS FOR DIFFERENT CONDITIONS

TREES AND SHRUBS FOR SCREENING PURPOSES

*E = Evergreen   * = Spreading   Vars. = Varietes of   ! = Upright*

	Proper names	Common name	Habit Width	Height	Comments
E	*Arundinaria* vars.	Bamboo	3–4.5m (10–15ft)		*
E	*Berberis stenophylia*	Barberry	2.1–2.7m (7–9ft)		*
	Betula vars.	Birch	3.6–15m (12–50ft)		!
E	*Cedrus deodara*	Deodar	15–27m (50–89ft)		*
E	*Cotoneaster cornubia*		4.5–7.5m (15–24½ft)		*
E	*Cryptomeria elegans*	Japanese cedar	7.5–12m (24½–40ft)		*
E	*Cupressocyparis leylandii*	Leyland cypress	15–27m (49–89ft)		*!
E	*Cupressus macrocarpa 'Lutea'*	Monterey cypress	7.5–12m (24½–39ft)		!
E	*Elaeagnus ebbingei*		1.5–2.1m (5–7ft)		*
E	*Escallonia* vars.		1.2–3m (4–10ft)		*
E	*Eucalyptus* vars.	Gum tree	12–27m (39–89ft)		!
E	*Ligustrum* vars.	Privet	2.1–3.3m (7–11ft)		*
E	*Pinus nigricans*	Austrian pine	12–21m (40–69ft)		*
	Polygonum baldschuanicum	Russian vine	4.5–9m (15–30ft)		* Climber
	Populus nigra 'Italica'	Lombardy poplar	18–27m (59–89ft)		!
	Prunus avium	Bird cherry	7.5–13.5m (24½–45ft)		*
E	*Prunus laurocerasus*	Laurel	3–5.4m (10–18ft)		*
	Prunus pissardii	Pissard's purple-leaved plum	4.5–7.5m (15–24½ft)		*
E	*Pyracantha* vars.	Firethorn	2.7–4.8m (9–16ft)		*
E	*Rhododendron ponticum*		4.5–7.5m (15–24½ft)		*
	Rosa 'Frühlingsgold'		1.8–3.6m (6–12ft)		*
	Sorbus aria 'Lutescens'	Mountain ash	6–12m (20–40ft)		!
E	*Thuya plicata*	Arbor-vitae	7.5–13.5m (24½–45ft)		*

TREES AND SHRUBS SHADED WALLS

*E = Evergreen   * = Spreading   Vars. = Varietes of   ! = Upright*

	Proper names	Common name	Habit Width	Height	Comments
E	*Berberis × stenophylla*	Barberry	2.7m (9ft)		*
E	*Camellia* vars.		1.5–2.4m (5–8ft)		*
	Chaenomeles vars.	Flowering quince	2.1–4.5m (7–15ft)		*
	Choisya ternata		6–9m (20–30ft)		*
	Clematis montana		6–9m (20–30ft)		* Climber
	Cotoneaster horizontalis		0.3–0.37m (1–1¼ft)		*
	Daphne mezereum		1–1.5m (3¼–5ft)		!
E	*Euonymus fortunei* vars.		0.6–1.8m (2–6ft)		*
	Garrya eliptica	Silk tassel bush	2.7m (9ft)		*
	Hydrangea petiolaris		9–15m (30–50ft)		* Climber
	Jasminum nudiflorum		4.5–6m (15–20ft)		* Climber
E	*Mahonia japonica*		1.8–3m (6–10ft)		!
	Parthenocissus vars.	Virginia creeper	6–12m (20–40ft)		* Climber
E	*Pyracantha* vars.	Firethorn	2.7–4.8m (9–16ft)		*

TREES AND SHRUBS SHADE-TOLERANT

E = Evergreen   * = Spreading   B = Bulb   ! = Upright
VARS = Varieties of   HP = Herbaceous perennial

	Proper names	Common name	Width	Height	Comments
	Arundinaria vars.	Bamboo	3–4.5m (10–15ft)		*
E	*Aucuba* vars.	Spotted laurel	1.5–2.7m (5–9ft)		*
E	*Berberis* vars.	Barberry	0.45–1.8m (1½–6ft)		*
	Bergenia vars.		0.3m (1ft)		*
E	*Camellia* vars.		1.5–2.4m (5–8ft)		*
	Chaenomeles vars.		2.1–4.5m (7–15ft)		*
	Clethra alnifolia	White alder	2.7–4.5m (9–15ft)		*
	Cornus alba 'Sibirica'	Dogwood	1.2–2.4m (4–8ft)		*
	Corylopsis vars.	Winter hazel	0.9–4.5m (3–15ft)		*
	Cotoneaster horizontalis		0.3–0.9m (1–3ft)		* 1.8–2.4m (6–8ft) (as wall shrub)
B	*Cyclamen* vars.		0.1–0.15m (4–6in)		*
E	*Danaë racemosa*	Alexandrian laurel	0.6–0.9m (2–3ft)		*
	Daphne mezereum	Mezereon	1.5–2.4m (5–8ft)		*
	Deutzia vars.		1.2–2.1m (4–7ft)		*
	Disanthus cercidifolius		2.1–4.5m (7–15ft)		*
E	*Elaeagnus* vars.		1.8–2.7m (6–9ft)		*
	Enkianthus campanulatus		2.1–2.7m (7–9ft)		!
	Euonymus alatus	Spindle berry	2.1–2.7m (7–9ft)		*
HP	*Euphorbia robbiae*	Spurge	0.45–0.6m (1½–2ft)		*
E	*Fatsia japonica*	Fig-leaf palm	1.2–2.1m (4–7ft)		*
E	*Gaultheria shallon*		1.5–2.1m (5–7ft)		*
E	*Hedera* vars.	Ivy	4.5–12m (15–40ft)		* Climber
HP	*Helleborus* vars.	Hellebore	0.6m (2ft)		*
HP	*Hosta* vars.	Plantain lily	0.6–0.75m (2–2½ft)		*
	Hydrangea vars.		0.6–2.7m (2–9ft)		*
	Hypericum calycinum	St John's wort	0.15–0.22m (6–8½in)		*
B	*Iris foetidissima*	Gladwyn iris	0.45–0.6m (1½–2ft)		*
HP	*Lamium maculatum* 'Beacon Silver'	Spotted dead nettle	0.15m (6in)		*
	Leucothoë catesbaei		0.9–1.8m (3–6ft)		*
E	*Ligustrum* vars.	Privet	2.1–3.3m (7–11ft)		*
	Liriope muscari		0.3–0.45m (1–1½ft)		*
E	*Mahonia* vars.		0.45–1.5m (1½–5ft)		*
E	*Pachysandra terminalis*		0.15–0.22m (6–8½in)		*
E	*Pieris* vars.	Lily-of-the-valley	1.8–6m (6–20ft)		*
HP	*Polygonatum* × *hybridum*	Solomon's seal	0.75–0.9m (2½–3ft)		*
E	*Prunus laurocerasus* 'Otto Luyken'		0.9m (3ft)		*
E	*Pyracantha* vars.	Firethorn	2.7–4.8m (9–16ft)		*
E	*Rhododendron* vars.		0.3–6m (1–20ft)		*!
	Rubus vars.		2.1–2.7m (7–9ft)		*
E	*Ruscus aculeatus*	Butcher's broom	0.6–0.9m (2–3ft)		!
E	*Sarcococca* vars.	Sweet box	0.37–0.6m (1¼–2ft)		*
HPE	*Saxifraga umbrosa*	London pride	0.3–0.45m (1–1½ft)		*

	Proper names	Common name	Habit Width–Height	Comments
E	Skimmia vars.	Spotted laurel	0.9–1.5m (3–5ft)	*
	Symphoricarpos vars.	Snowberry	1.2–1.8m (4–6ft)	
E	Taxus baccata	Yew	12–18m (40–59ft)	!
	Vaccinium corymbosum	American blueberry	1.5–1.8m (5–6ft)	*
E	Vinca vars.	Periwinkle	0.15–0.45m (½–1½ft)	*

TREES AND SHRUBS FOR DRY, SUNNY POSITIONS

E = Evergreen * = Spreading Vars. = Varieties of ! = Upright

	Proper names	Common name	Habit Width	Habit Height	Comments
	Artemisia abrotanum	Southernwood/ Lad's love	0.6–1.2m (2–4ft)		*
E	Berberis vars.	Barberry	0.45–1.9m (1½–6¼ft)		*
	Buddleia vars.	Butterfly bush	1.8–3m (6–10ft)		*
E	Buxus vars.	Box	0.9–2.4m (3–8ft)		*
	Caryopteris clandonensis	Blue spiraea	0.45–0.75m (1½–2½ft)		*
	Ceratostigma willmottianum	Hardy plumbago	0.3–0.6m (1–2ft)		*
	Chaenomeles vars.	Flowering quince	2–4.5m (6½–15ft)		*
E	Cistus vars.	Rock rose	0.15–1.8m (½–6ft)		*
E	Convolvulus cneorum		0.45–0.6m (1½–2ft)		*
	Cytisus vars.	Broom	0.45–1.8m (1½–6ft)		*
E	Erica vars.	Heather	0.15–2.4m (½–8ft)		*!
E	Euonymus vars.	Spindle berry	0.45–2.4m (1½–8ft)		*
	Fuchsia vars.		0.9–2m (3–6½ft)		*
	Genista hispanica	Spanish gorse	0.45–0.6m (1½–2ft)		*
	Hedysarum vars.	French honeysuckle	0.9–1.2m (3–4ft)		*
	Hibiscus vars.	Rose mallow	2–4m (6½–13ft)		!
	Hypericum vars.	St John's wort	0.15–1.2m (½–4ft)		*
E	Lavandula vars.	Lavender	0.45–0.9m (1½–3ft)		*
	Lavatera olbia	Tree mallow	1.5–2.4m (5–8ft)		*
	Lupinus arboreus	Tree lupin	1.2–2m (4–6½ft)		*
	Lycium chinensis	Box thorn	1.5–2m (5–6½ft)		*
E	Olearia vars.	Daisy bush	0.9–1.5m (3–5ft)		*
	Potentilla fruticosa	Shrubby cinquefoil	0.35–1.5m (14in–5ft)		*
	Rhus cotinus	Smoke bush	2.7–4.5m (9–15ft)		*
	Robinia pseudoacacia	False acacia	9–15m (30–50ft)		!
	Rosa vars.		Variable		
E	Rosmarinus vars.	Rosemary	0.15–1.8m (½–6ft)		*!
E	Santolina incana	Cotton lavender	0.35–0.9m (14in–3ft)		*
E	Senecio greyi		0.9–1.5m (3–5ft)		*
	Spartium junceum	Spanish broom	1.8–2.4m (6–8ft)		*
	Tamarix tetrandra	Tamarisk	2.5–3m (8¼–10ft)		*
	Ulex europaeus	Gorse	1.2–2.4m (4–8ft)		*
E	Vinca vars.	Periwinkle	0.1–0.15m (4–6in)		*
E	Yucca vars.		1.5–3m (5–10ft)		!

PLANTS SUITABLE FOR CONTAINERS

E = Evergreen * = Spreading HH = Half Hardy Vars. = Varieties of
! = Upright C = Climber HP = Herbaceous Perennial

	Proper names	Common name	Habit Width	Height	Comments
	Abutilon megapotamicum		1.8–2.4m (6–8ft)		HH C
	Acer palmatum vars., e.g. 'Dissectum Atropurpureum'		1.5–2.4m (5–8ft)		*
E	Arundinaria vars.	Bamboo	0.9–2.4m (3–8ft)		*!
E	Aucuba japonica vars.	Spotted laurel	1.5–2.4m (5–8ft)		*
E	Camellia vars.		1.8–2.4m (6–8ft)		*
E	Chamaecyparis lawsoniana vars., e.g. 'Ellwood's Gold'		2.4–3.6m (8–12ft)		*!
E	Choisya ternata	Mexican orange blossom	1.8–2.4m (6–8ft)		*
E	Cordyline australis	Cabbage palm	3.6–9m (12–30ft)		*!
E	Cryptomeria japonica vars.	Japanese cedar	2m (6½ft) upward		*!
	Cytisus vars.	Broom	0.5m (1¾ft) upward		
E	Elaeagnus pungens 'Maculata'		2.4–3m (8–10ft)		*
E	Escallonia vars.		1.8m (6ft)		*
E	× Fatshedera lizei		0.6–0.9m (2–3ft)		*
E	Fatsia japonica	Fig-leaf palm	2.4–3.6m (8–12ft)		*
	Fuchsia vars.		0.6–0.9m (2–3ft)		*
	Genista lydia		0.45–0.75m (1½–2½ft)		
	Hibiscus syriacus	Tree hollyhock	2.1–3m (7–10ft)		
	Hydrangea vars.		0.9–1.8m (3–6ft)		
E	Juniperus communis 'Compressa'	Common juniper	0.6–0.9m (2–3ft)		!
E	Juniperus virginiana 'Skyrocket'	Pencil cedar	3–3.5m (10–11½ft)		!
E	Laurus nobilis	Bay laurel	1.5–1.8m (5–6ft)		*
	Miniature roses		0.3m (1ft)		
E	Myrtus communis	Common myrtle	2.4–3m (8–10ft)		HH *
E	Phormium tenax	New Zealand flax	1–2m (3¼–6½ft)		
E	Rhododendrons and azaleas		0.9–1.8m (3–6ft)		
E	Rosmarinus officinalis	Rosemary	1.2–1.8m (4–6ft)		
E	Viburnum tinus		1.8–3m (6–10ft)		*
E	Yucca gloriosa		1–3m (3¼–10ft)		!

PLEASE NOTE: All plants in containers require additional watering even during wet weather.

TREES AND SHRUBS FOR TOWN GARDENS (POLLUTION RESISTANT!)

E = *Evergreen*   * = *Spreading*   Vars. = *Varieties of*   ! = *Upright*

	Proper names	Common name	Habit Width	Height	Comments
	Acer vars.	Maple	1.2–15m (4–50ft)		* !
	Aesculus hippocastanum	Horse chestnut	12–18m (40–59ft)		*
	Ailanthus altissima	Tree of heaven	15–21m (50–69ft)		!
	Berberis (deciduous vars.)	Barberry	0.45–1.8m (1½–6ft)		*
	Betula vars.	Birch	3.6–4.5m (12–15ft)		* !
	Buddleia vars.	Butterfly bush	1.8–3m (6–10ft)		*
	Chaenomeles vars.	Flowering quince	2.1–4.5m (7–15ft)		*
	Cornus vars.	Dogwood	1.8–6m (6–20ft)		*
	Cotoneaster vars.		0.37–2.4m (1¼–8ft)		*
	Crataegus vars.		4.5–7.5m (15–24½ft)		*
	Dahne mezereum	Mezereon	1.5–2.4m (5–8ft)		*
	Deutzia vars.		1.2–2.1m (4–7ft)		*
E	*Euonymus radicans*	Spindle berry	0.15–0.3m (½–1ft)		*
E	*Fatsia japonica*	Fig-leaf palm	1.2–2.1m (4–7ft)		*
E	*Forsythia* vars.		2.1–4.5m (7–15ft)		*
E	*Hedera* vars.	Ivy	4.5–12m (15–40ft)		* Climber
	Hibiscus vars.	Rose mallow	2.1–4.2m (7–14ft)		!
	Hypericum vars.	St John's wort	0.15–1.2m (½–4ft)		*
	Jasminum vars.	Jasmine	2.4–4.2m (8–14ft)		*
	Kerria japonica	Jew's mallow	1.2–1.8m (4–6ft)		*
	Laburnum × vossii	Golden chain	3.6–6m (12–20ft)		!
E	*Ligustrum* vars.	Privet	2.1–3.3m (7–11ft)		*
E	*Mahonia* vars.		0.45–1.5m (1½–5ft)		*
	Malus vars.	Crab apple	4.5–7.5m (15–24½ft)		*
E	*Olearia × haastii*	Daisy bush	1.2–1.8m (4–6ft)		*
E	*Parthenocissus quinquefolia*	Virginia creeper	3.6–12m (12–40ft)		*
E	*Pernettya* vars.	Prickly heath	0.6–1.5m (2–5ft)		*
	Philadelphus vars.	Mock orange	1.8–4.5m (6–15ft)		*
	Prunus vars.	Flowering cherry	2.7–7.5m (9–24½ft)		* !
E	*Pyracantha* vars.	Firethorn	2.7–4.8m (9–16ft)		*
	Rhus typhina	Sumach	2.4–4.5m (8–15ft)		*
	Ribes sanguineum	Flowering currant	1.8–2.4m (6–8ft)		!
	Rosa vars.		Variable		
E	*Senecio greyi*		0.9–1.5m (3–5ft)		*
	Sorbus vars.		0.9–7.5m (3–24½ft)		!
	Spiraea vars.		0.45–1.2m (1½–4ft)		*
	Syringa vars.	Lilac	0.45–3m (1½–10ft)		* !
E	*Veronica traversii*	Shrubby speedwell	1.2–1.5m (4–5ft)		*
	Viburnum vars.		1.2–2.1m (4–7ft)		*
E	*Vinca* vars.	Periwinkle	0.1–0.15m (4–6in)		*
	Weigela vars.		1.5–2.1m (5–7ft)		*
E	*Yucca* vars.		1.8–3m (6–10ft)		!

USEFUL ADDRESSES

The Landscape Institute

is the professional body for landscape architects, landscape managers and landscape scientists. It maintains a list of Registered landscape practices and also provides career information.
For further information write to:
The Registrar
The Landscape Institute
12 Carlton House Terrace
London SW1Y 5AH

The Society of Landscape and Garden Designers

can provide a list of its members, all of whom have had to demonstrate their competence before joining.
A list of accredited landscape and design courses is also available on written request from:
The Honorary Secretary
The Society of Landscape and Garden Designers
23 Reigate Road
Ewell
Surrey KT17 1PS

Magazines offering postal design services include:
Homes & Gardens
House Beautiful
Practical Gardening
Good Housekeeping

For information about gardens belonging to
The National Gardens Scheme
write to:
The National Gardens Scheme
Hatchlands Park
East Clandon
Guildford
Surrey GU4 7RT

PEOPLE AND SUPPLIERS INVOLVED IN THE JONES'S GARDEN

Designer
Julie Toll
44 Sefton Road
Stevenage
Herts SG1 5RJ

Contractors
Brambles Garden Services
126 Winford Drive
Broxbourne
Herts EN10 6PW

Fencing
Lap panel:
Larch-Lap Ltd
P.O. Box 17
Stourport-on-Severn
Worcs DY13 9ES

Conservatory
Victorian-style, octagonal-shaped Amblestone conservatory:
Strand Conservatories
Windsor House
Trent Valley Road
Lichfield
Staffs WS13 6EE

Grass
Rolawn Medallion Turf:
Rolawn Ltd are growers and suppliers of cultivated turf and have depots nationwide

Brick, paving and walling
Butterfields Woburn Blend facing brick:
H. Butterfield Ltd
Builders' Merchants
Selbourne Road
Luton
Beds LU4 8QF

Paving
Bradstone Wetherdale paving:
H. Butterfield Ltd
(as above)

Irrigation
Purpose-built watering system:
H₂O Irrigation Ltd (Bournemouth
8 Alridge Road
Ferndown
Dorset BH22 8LT

Barbecue
Odell U-Build-It barbecue:
Frank Odell Ltd
70 High Street
Teddington
Middlesex TW11 8JD

Bark mulch
Forest bark:
ICI Garden and Professional Products
Woolmead House East
Woolmead Walk
Farnham
Surrey GU9 7UB

Conservatory Furniture
supplied by Marks & Spencer p

Garden Shed
Van Hage's Garden Centre
Great Amwell
Nr Ware
Herts SG12 9RP

INDEX

Page numbers in *italic* refer to the illustrations.

111

INDEX

Suppliers for the Instant Garden seen on television
Automatic watering by Gardena UK Ltd
Metal features by Peter Betton Ltd
Stocbord coloured flooring by Plastic Recycling Ltd a Superwood Group Company
Multigrip cladding rail for mesh surround by Fordingbridge Engineering Ltd
Mesh netting surround by Netlon Ltd
Glass nuggets by House of Marbles
Fashioned growbag by The Exceptional Bag Company
Roller climber support by Apollo Window Blinds
Plants by Jardinerie Ltd
Construction by Premier Landscapes